VOLUME SIX OF THE

YALE EDITION OF THE

UNPUBLISHED WRITINGS OF

GERTRUDE STEIN

under the general editorship

of Carl Van Vechten

with an advisory committee of

Donald Gallup,

Donald Sutherland,

and Thornton Wilder

THE YALE EDITION OF THE

UNPUBLISHED WRITINGS OF GERTRUDE STEIN

Two: Gertrude Stein and Her Brother

Mrs. Reynolds and Five Earlier Novelettes

Bee Time Vine and Other Pieces (1913–1927)

As Fine as Melanctha (1914–1930)

Painted Lace and Other Pieces (1914–1937)

Stanzas in Meditation and Other Poems (1929–1933)

STANZAS IN MEDITATION

AND OTHER POEMS [1929–1933]

BY GERTRUDE STEIN

with a Preface by Donald Sutherland

NEW HAVEN: YALE UNIVERSITY PRESS

London: Geoffrey Cumberlege, Oxford University Press

1956

PREFACE: THE TURNING POINT

By Donald Sutherland

The works in the present volume were written between 1929 and 1933, one of the most dramatic periods in Gertrude Stein's long life with literary form. The period was in a way the climax of her heroic experimentation with the essentials of writing; it tired her, and after it came her popular, broader and easier, more charming and personal works, but while the period lasted she carried writing as high and as far in her direction as she could, to a point that is still, over twenty years later, a crucial one for writing in general. Her summit of innovation, this last reach of her dialectic, is not easy of approach, the atmosphere is rare, but even the approaches are exhilarating and it is not difficult at least to map out the region and the way she came, much of it being our own ground at present.

In the preceding period, from 1911 to 1928, she had written about things and people in space—on the analogy of painting or the theatre. She had done so naturally, as that period was great in painting and lively in the theatre, and nearly everybody's writing was controlled by imagery. The spatial existence of anything made it real enough to write about and indeed to sustain the existence of the writing, but then something happened—even before the crash of 1929 and the small and large world events after it—something happened that took the sufficiency out of spatial existence. Painting went literary, even the movies began to talk, and writing abandoned imagery gradually for other kinds of reality, especially discourse. Why this all happened I

don't know, but it did, and set up a situation I believe still remains
to be resolved, both in theory and in practice. It goes something
like this:

The mind—that is, the active, live, and most actual meaning—
of a written work manifests itself in the ways it treats three ma-
terials: sight, sound, and sense, as Gertrude Stein counted them.
They can as well be called the pictorial, musical, and ideal elements, or again, the spatial, temporal, and conceptual, but however roughly they may be distinguished a writer usually feels only
one of them to represent the foremost face of natural reality and
make the sharpest challenge to the mind, which means to make
what it does at least as real to itself as the natural or given world.
This one leading material or dimension assures the adequate reality
of the work, while the other two may serve to reinforce, or re-
fresh, or accompany, or arm, the mind in its major action upon
the primary element. For some plain examples: In Pope the sense
is primary or the authenticating element, while the sight and
sound are there for emphasis and ornament, to help what oft
was thought be well expressed or dressed; in Swinburne the sound
—the whole musicality of rhythm and rhyme—is primary, while
the sense and sight are embellishments; and in say Amy Lowell
the sight is everything while the sound and sense are as may be.
A similar prevalence of one element over others happens within
the art of painting, where the validating element will be now line,
now color, now volume, etc.; and within music, where it will be
now melody, now harmony, now rhythm.

One might, with a preference for stability over excitement,
like to place the excellence of a written work in an equal force
or balance of sight, sound, and sense at once, but the trouble (or
the mercy, if you prefer) is that rarely if ever in any historical
period is experience lived equally in terms of space, time, and
ideas, though of course they are always together in experience
in some proportion or other. If the period is tranquil the sense of
time is likely to be less vivid than the sense of objects in space; if
the period is violent and changeable the sense of time will dominate. Sometimes the rationality of the universe is convincing
enough and sometimes the irrationality of it is more so, so thought
as the validating element in writing comes and goes.

Actual periods are of course more complex than that, as many writers work counter to their period in some way or degree, and the spatiality of writing in the period 1911 to 1928 was in part a counter to what was left of the late 19th century sense of time as history or even biology moving vastly on through a universe which was, if not rational, at least scientifically minded. So time and ideas were still interesting, but they had become problematical, indeed an annoyance to not a few, and all sorts of games could be played with them, while space was a given and saving reality, even to Proust and Joyce, as well as to Gertrude Stein.

But in about 1928 the general sense of the authenticity of space weakened. The pictorial element in writing, which had been highly evolved technically, continued of its own inertia, but it continued rather as decoration or illustration or symbol, because at this time writing began to base its reality on thought.

Most of the thought was political or religious or philosophical. T. S. Eliot went that way; so did Pound; Auden and that generation arrived, all bristling with ideas. Some absconse erudition and some Freudian apparatus did still hang on, passing for thought and even sounding like it, but I believe most of the thought was direct, fresh, and contemporary, really rousing at the time. Only, an idea that is exciting to live with rarely stays exciting long when written, supposing it even begins to be exciting enough for writing of such high intensity as poetry: it is awful what quantities of that poetry, written with a content of the most urgent ideas, are now no longer so much as curious, because the ideas were incompletely converted into the subjective continuum of poetry, and the pressing objective context which kept them alive for a time has withdrawn into history and left them stranded. So much of that poetry, being *about* ideas and not instinct with the poetry *of* ideas, has turned out parochial or didactic in the deplorable sense.

Gertrude Stein once said there were no ideas in masterpieces and next to no masterpieces in philosophy, yet at this time she felt, like everybody else, the need of ideas in writing, as experience was composing itself predominantly into issues, not states or events as before. But she knew very well that ideas had to be made intrinsic to poetry, made to exist as poetry, not used as external props, as occasions or justifications of poetry as if philosophy or religion or politics could delegate some of their authority and interest to poetry while remaining themselves and outside it.

Sight and sound are more readily assimilable than sense from the reality of experience into the reality of poetry: being sensory and particular they need bring little or no reference or association with them and can belong more closely than ideas to the actuality and specific form of the poem. Sound indeed, as rhyme and rhythm, can belong to the poem alone, and anyone prefers the auditory effects to stay inside the poem. One is ultimately annoyed or amused by onomatopoeia for example or say the use of spondees for something big or heavily moving in the subject matter; one likes the sound to be so far as possible self-contained, like "pure" music, a continuity of character or expression by itself, at most to follow the general emotion of the poem over the subject matter, and never but in passing or as an amiable concession to illustrate the objective behavior of the subject matter.

The same is almost as true of sight. In a thorough poem the actual look of the words on the page does count, but hardly as rhythm and rhyme do (except when, as with E. E. Cummings, it is deliberately made to), and sight is mainly a slightly less actual matter: imagery. Though the word is directly seen and the image is imagined, still the image is more actual than the idea. An image, like a concrete natural phenomenon, is "realized" by the intuition, whereas ideas are realized by reference, either to phenomena or to other ideas. An image, unless it is used as a symbol, is entirely there to the imagination, as an object is to the eye. Its primary relations can be not to the rest of natural reality from which it is drawn but to other images within the poem, making a kind of pictorial composition, or to the central emotion or key quality of the whole poem or passage. When Tennyson calls a falling stream a "downward smoke" or Hopkins speaks of "rose moles all in stipple upon trout that swim" the imagery is, on reflection, true enough to waterfalls and trout, but truer to the quality of the poems—to the languor of "The Lotus Eaters" in one case and to the exhaustive and bursting splendor of "Pied Beauty" in the other. So imagery can actualize and realize itself within the continuity of the poem, more or less completely, but it is hard to keep an idea, which is essentially a reference, from sticking out of the continuity, less like a sore thumb than like an index finger, directing the reader elsewhere. It is quite reasonable to despair of ideas for poetry; Cocteau could say poetry stops at the idea; and if poetry is essentially something and ideas are essentially about something not themselves, that seems to be that.

All the same, at the time, ideas were needed, and it came to Gertrude Stein, more clearly, I think, than to others, that after all grammar and rhetoric are in themselves actualizations of ideas and the beginning, perhaps, of a conversion of ideas into poetry, since they are in their way shapes or schemes, aesthetic configurations, even if not commonly felt to be so. The epigrammatic style of the 18th century, with its closed couplets, its balances, points, and antitheses, is not officially well thought of, but it was a partial solution to this problem. Other solutions had come long ago, when the articulation of general ideas was still a new game, after Homer, and even Sappho and Pindar felt the junctures of discourse as aesthetic schemes—not to mention the poets called or miscalled didactic, and of course Plato. But grammar and rhetoric degenerate into techniques of exposition and persuasion, into ustensility and functionalism, ceasing to be the marvelous shapes or intellectual dance steps they were earlier.

The ancient distinction between the literary effects Persuasion and Ecstasy is good for distinguishing the effects of ideas in writing. In most of our writing ideas are meant to persuade, an inferior effect, and it is very hard to make them rise into ecstasy, even with elegance and grace and tensility and musicality in the rhetorical and syntactical figures. But that was what Gertrude Stein was trying to do in such works as "Stanzas in Meditation," and though I think she frequently succeeded, only time will tell with any sort of persuasion.

Time has persuaded us that something of this kind can be done in poetry, the plainest tradition being perhaps the Pindaric, from Pindar through Horace and Ronsard, the English Metaphysicals, even Wordsworth, and certainly Hopkins in "The Wreck of the Deutschland." This is not to say that the ideas of Milton, Dryden, and Pope, or of Wordsworth outside his one great ode, of Byron, and Shelley, or of many others—of Dante in particular whose excellence in using "the operations of the human mind" as poetical figures Shelley pointed out—never rise out of persuasion; but the full lyricity of ideas * is, I think, more markedly and deliberately sustained in the Pindaric tradition, usually in the special form of the *ode*. The ode is usually full of ideas, but not composed in their logical or persuasive connections, rather disengaged from these deliberately, in order to have the quality of a vivid sudden willful happening, not that of a docile or mechanical consequence. This "beau désordre," as Boileau called it, is native to the ode, making it the natural vehicle for the lyricity of ideas.

In the ode and in poetry of the kind the delight is mainly in the movement and accent of phrasing as the syntactical and rhetorical figures are played on or against or over the lines and metric, and, in case of rhyme, the rhymes. In Pindar the subject matter—the winners at the games and so on—is there but perfunctory, and occasional, rather a point of departure than a topic, and this bold preference in such writers for the movement and life of ideas as they actually eventuate in writing, over the claims of the exterior subject, leads, typically, to such phenomena as the conceits of the Metaphysicals, where the acrobatic performance of the ideas is most of their meaning, or to the splendid commonplaces of classical poetry, whose "truth" as often as not is strictly confined to the mind of the poem (e.g. "Whatever is is right" or "Nessun maggior dolore," etc.) or to the Romantic exclamation of abstractions (e.g. "O World! O Life! O Time!"). For practical purposes these phenomena may be irrelevant or confusing or worse, but not for the most serious artistic purpose, which takes thought as an art form when not merely as raw material, much as mathematics can be so taken, whether the systems correspond to a reality outside themselves or not—the ecstasy of their intrinsic beauty being their "cash value." Plato, a poet and mathematician as well as a philosopher, could feel that way about ideas, calling philosophy a kind of music, dedicating his Academy to the Muses, and, once out of patience with another philosopher who was very earnest about ideas but less an artist in them than himself, telling him to sacrifice to the Graces.

But the essential motive for absorbing ideas into an art form

* I mean *liricità* as in Croce, who moreover describes the process of lyricizing ideas in Dante.

(whether poems or fables or parables or plays or prose romances) is to repossess and revive in the subjective and living time of the human mind those concluded, inert, objective utensils which ideas become, once the mind has constructed them, for practical purposes, as accounts or maps of objective reality—or as tools or "weapons" for dealing with it. An idea is not ours and not alive unless it is essentially an event or part of an episode in human thinking, unless it occurs in a subjectivity. An idea that is alive and absorbing one year, say, because it relates to the main and active interests of the subjectivity at that time, is, the next year, only a fact or an object, sound asleep if not permanently dead, unless it is, by art, made to be a fresh event in a continuum of subjectivity, that is, the poem, the mime, the romance, or whatever. Outside of art the past idea has only an historical or academic interest, until it strikes the peculiar sympathies of a later period as all but contemporary with it and alive, but even then it has a zombie or somnambulant quality. The merely exposed and objectively articulated ideas of Aristotle and Saint Thomas, for example, whether true or not, exude that horror, and it takes all of Dante to make them sweet. While the dramatized ideas of Plato, even if less true for us, are still as fresh as daisies—so long, at least, as they are left in the dialogues.

In her way Gertrude Stein solved the problem of keeping ideas in their primary life, that is, of making them events in a subjective continuum of writing, of making them completely actual. For one thing, the ideas she uses, in "Stanzas," are about the actual writing before one, sometimes about her previous writing, other people's writing, or the ordinary events of her life at the time of writing. So the writing is, insofar as it is about anything, about ideas about writing, and this reflexive or so to say circular reference of the ideas is one way of making them self-contained and, while moving certainly, absolute. She was interested at this time in composition as something folded upon itself or contained in itself, and here the movement and reference of the ideas make such a thing. By taking as her center of reference the actual writing rather than writing in general, she gains a greater immediacy and completeness than other works on much the same scheme—the *Ars Poetica* of Horace, that of Boileau, that of Verlaine, and so on.

While one can, with the requisite attention, follow the movements of the ideas among or against each other and in relation to the verse, the very tense and elegant behavior of the syntax, she has so thoroughly suppressed the connections between these formal or verbal configurations of the ideas and any practical, theoretical, or historical context from which they have been abstracted that the work is at first bewildering. Often, yes, one can tell what the specific subject or occasion of a passage or stanza was, or make a sufficiently shrewd guess at the subject for the whole body of references to fall into place in history or philosophy, and take on an objective or extrinsic meaning, but this kind of clarity is, if a relief sometimes when it comes, really a temptation and a distraction from the actual aesthetic object. Gertrude Stein meant these lines of verse to be as attenuated and disembodied as the drawing of Francis Picabia—with whom a few of the stanzas are concerned (as pp. 145–6)—and who, she observed in *The Autobiography of Alice B. Toklas*, was in pursuit of "the vibrant line." Whether Picabia often captured it is a question, but a very good example of its capture would be the draughtsmanship of the Greek vase painter Exekias, if he were more familiar. At any rate, in a stanza concerning Picabia she says she told him to forget men and women—meaning that the line should become so intensely its own entity and sustained by an energy or "vibration" now intrinsic to it, that it could disengage itself from the character of the figures it began by bounding or delineating or expressing. Just so, she wanted her own writing —the grammatical sequence, the rhetorical figures, the line of discourse—to disengage itself by virtue of its own intensity of assertion from the concrete or specific situation whose articulation or definition or "bounding" was precisely the genesis of the idea in the form of a statement, a proposition, a sentence, a word, or whatever.

But can the "lyricity" of ideas really be made to fly, to transcend its origins and their references to any such degree, even if drawing sometimes can? Perhaps not, but I think anyone can see that a writer could passionately want it to be done—to go on, so to say, where Pindar and Plato left off, and create a continuum of absolute writing or absolute thought in words as it can be created in numbers. The audacity of the attempt in itself is staggering, and the difficulty was exhausting. Gertrude Stein finally gave it up and turned to writing about historical relations, and even the easier way out that symbolism is, though she indulged in it not very often.

(In "Stanzas" she does, if infrequently, use symbolism or a degree of it, metaphor: the first line of the first stanza is "I caught a bird that made a ball"—meaning "I captured a 'lyricity' that constituted a complete and self-contained entity." Such figures are not typical of what the work generally is or does. Her express attitude toward symbolism was to refuse it as such but to allow in theory and sometimes to practice what she called "symbolical literature"—apparently a literature containing symbolical imagery as above, but an imagery created for the sake of its character in the immediate composition, not for the sake of such a meaning as I have deciphered above. Symbolization would then be a method, like abstraction, of transmuting raw material into art, and not meant to "signify" the raw material—which is, like Picabia's "men and women," to be forgotten. This is theoretically all very well, and I admit that symbols provide a richness, a substantive weight, and some color in a perhaps too purely linear style, if they are taken literally as images and not interpreted, but they inevitably tempt one into interpretation, or me they do, and I mistrust them both in theory and in practice. I find them too interesting and not exciting enough. But a reader who can take them as they are meant—literally, as images and nouns—may well find they help to brace and sustain the "vibration" instead of interrupting it. However one feels about symbols, they are not, in this work, many.)

One of her difficulties was the fluidity of English, the invertebrate sequence and blur of overtones it has in normal use. Its Latin element is no longer a structural or linear resource, but mainly color or pedal, and at one point in the stanzas she longs for Italian, wishing "Italian had been wiser," that is, no doubt, that the superb rhetorical buoyancy and sharpness of Italian had not gone flaccid and indiscriminate as it did after Dante—or Tasso at the latest. Shelley could still use the "clear and complete language of Italy" as spoken or sung, for a foil or scale against which to make English even more fluid than it is, but current Italian is not the help it might have been in forcing English, saturated as it is with the indeterminate concreteness of the English mind, to the expression of what Gertrude Stein called with abundant reason the abstractness of the American mind. The clarity and completeness of Italian might help, but its lusciousness, which afflicted even Dante who invented the language, spoils when brought into American severity, rawness, edginess, what you will. Spanish is more promising, and Hemingway tried it, but something goes wrong there too. The only consolation is that translations of Gertrude Stein and imitations of Hemingway make excellent Italian literature. The real problem, of how to get a foreign language like English to express the exact tone and accent and movement of the American mind, still remains, and one may attach considerable importance to this most heroic attempt to solve it.

The above makes it sound like a laboratory and rather a grim go, which it is not. Gertrude Stein sacrificed to the Graces, and in the course of the "Stanzas" we have a good deal of comedy, general gayety, and such companionable remarks to the reader as "Thank you for hurrying through" or "I could go on with this." I have not, myself, seen all there is in the "Stanzas," far from it, nor all of what they are, but there is a luxuriance of pleasures waiting for almost any reader who is willing to enter into the "Stanzas" and stay a while. They are far more hospitable than they may at first appear.

The frugality of imagery will seem less forbidding if the reader sees that imagery was just what had to be reduced or liquidated at the time, in order to clarify the draughtsmanship of ideas, or if he recalls Dryden and the Metaphysicals when they are operating on the bare articulation of the language and the verse, with a minimum of coloristic or affective flourish. I think we now have to make some such effort, some deliberate tuning or focusing of the attention, since more recent poetry has disinterred if not revived imagery, in the lurider colors of its disintegration.

It may also require effort now to face a long philosophical poem, but the form was, oddly, of the period, as Bridges' *The Testament of Beauty* appeared then, Pound's *Cantos* were being written, and, on a smaller scale, T. S. Eliot's *Four Quartets*. Gertrude Stein's style and purpose have little enough in common with these poems, or with *The Excursion* or with *In Memoriam*, but the "Stanzas" do, by their general form, belong both to a fashion and to the tradition of the long, rambling, discursive poem whose interest and energy are primarily in the movement of the poet's mind writing.

A continuum of discourse, or of *sense* on its own, has a *sound*, an intrinsic musicality of its own, not only as Plato called philosophy a kind of music but as the ideas eventuate or evolve and move in the articulated time of the poem, so such poems are naturally called *The Prelude* or *Cantos* or *Four Quartets;* and the continuum has a space of its own, not only the marked "space of time" that a canto or stanza is, or by imagery when there is any, but by the extensions of thought which sentences are. Gertrude Stein kept, from grade school, a passion for the diagramming of sentences, and in most of her styles she wrote sentences as a kind of diagram of thought. Her superb sense of syntax led her to use it as a kind of draughtsmanship, sometimes as the basis of a more flowing calligraphy, but in these Meditations rather as a "vibrant line" on the order of Picabia's or Exekias' or of that in much Byzantine painting. The intellectual space, rarely so reinforced by imagery and symbol as in Pound or Eliot, or by landscape as in Wordsworth, is both a matter of the stanza—as literally a "room" —and of the extent of the sentence, doubled or further articulated by the extent of the line of verse. To be a little clearer about it: She had said that sentences are not emotional, paragraphs are— that is, that a sentence lives by the balance or tension of its internal syntactical structure (not by its words as successive events), but the paragraph lives by the succession and culmination of the sentences in it—and much the same quality and kind of organization hold for the relation of line to stanza. The line, like the sentence, is conceived as primarily structural, or diagrammatic, as it were spatial and all but static, while the succession of the lines making up the stanza is conceived as temporal. Her lines have, usually, the extremely dry and tense syntactical posture of the 18th century line, or, better, of the closed 18th century couplet, but the stanzas have the mounting and sumptuous progress to a fullness of say the Spenserian stanza or the Tasso octave. I think she would have said this is an American kind of composition, not unlike the sequence of units in a comic strip—in any case very unlike the Miltonic or Romantic permeation of lines by the syntax, where the periods are "variously drawn out from one verse into another."

The metric itself, usually a very plain iambic affair with reversed feet ad libitum as is normal in discursive English poetry, does not really move much through the lines but is rather a matter of immediate emphasis, a rhetorical accent rather than a properly temporal element, or musical. It is what one could call an intensive, as against a progressive, metric, and surely the commonest kind in modern poetry. And the words themselves, being preponderantly monosyllables, tend to stay put and not to progress, to stand or arrive intensively—to vibrate—but to contain no succession.

Still, if one likes, there is a syntactical *phrasing* as well as structure, and one could call that a musicality, like the succession of the sentences and lines, but even the phrasing is staccato and in any case both the temporality and the spatiality of the "Stanzas" are "ideal"—functions of the sense, of the articulate "thoughts" succeeding each other in a meditation. Though there are exceptions enough, I think this is true, that as a rule the "Stanzas" re-create a temporality and a spatiality out of the single ideal element, rather than taking them as separate and extrinsic elements brought in for the embellishment or reinforcement of the first. Thus they have little to do with real time and space, but are as it were native to the poem, functions of the moving and extending sense, as that sense moves upon or around itself.

It is high time for an example. Here is a relatively simple one, "Stanza VIII" in Part V:

> I wish now to wish now that it is now
> That I will tell very well
> What I think not now but now
> Oh yes oh yes now.
> What do I think now
> I think very well of what now
> What is it now it is this now
> How do you do how do you do
> And now how do you do now.
> This which I think now is this.

This stanza is more readily glossed than most, and so not a fair example of disembodied sense, but the form is easier to appreciate perhaps against so plain and immediate a meaning. The poem expresses the action of the mind willing and realizing its own presence, in the present, to its own thought. It begins by recognizing that the actual present is the time to tell one's thought, in the very instant of thinking (not, for example, that the present is to be used for preliminaries and plans for expressing the results of one's present or past thinking later on, as is most common with methodical thought). Then there come various exclamations, questions, and greetings to the present, and the resolution of the question and effort in a recognition that what the mind is present to in its act of presence is simply the *thisness* of any object.

The meaning, or so much of it, can be further discoursed and commented upon by the reader, to the effect that, yes, the nowness and thisness of a thought, not its connections with past or future thoughts or with an objective context of thoughts, are the conditions of its life, and of thought generally at its most vibrant. Plato's dialogues, when the thoughts are instantaneous in the conversation (and not, as, alas, they often are, simply exposition disguised as interrupted monologue), and Montaigne's essays, where the thoughts are explicitly just passing events in his Grand Central of a mind or only valid for the passing moment and not even for the next essay, would seem to agree. Contrariwise one can meditate upon the thatness of objective thought, the beyondness of universalizing thought, or the thenness of historical and anthropological thought, as limitations to their interest. Such excursions into the factual and philosophical context from which the "Stanzas" were drawn, abstracted and constructed, are a pleasure, and one can be sure that most if not all the ground one is likely to cover came within Gertrude Stein's immense knowledge of such matters; but excursions into the original context, however rich, do desert the intensiveness and immediacy of the abstracted thought as expressed. One should stay with the text, and yet the excursions do make one realize the amount of accepted material and value that Gertrude Stein sacrificed for the sake of an uncertain result, with an audacity of decision that marks the major poets, philosophers, saints, generals, and financiers.

The resultant and *intensive* meaning of these poems is the movement of the mind within the poem itself, and in this case the movement of thought, which is positive and active at every syllable, and so has a very high frequency and continuous immediacy, is further intensified by the extreme compression of phrase and the irreducible simplicity of vocabulary. This last, which is not unlike that of Plato, or Aristotle, or Seneca—or, better, that of Voltaire or Diderot or Hume—not only provides an elegant singleness of meaning word by word, thus adding to the tenseness and intensity, but also forces the expression to be a matter of syntax and rhetorical figure of a most linear kind, like a drawing done with a very fine stiff pen. With next to no sonority or harmonics the poems operate on sheer melodic shape, phrasing, and rhythm, other supports being only the bracing or balancing of the syntactical units on or over the line, the repetition of words and phrases, and a very spare use of internal rhyme —that much harmonics if you will. But it is all in a quite pure harpsichord manner.

The single lines are sometimes divided: by rhyme (as in "That I will tell very well"), by repetition (as in "How do you do how do you do"), and by question and answer (as in "What is it now it is this now"). Then there is a balancing or drawing taut of the line by repetition with differing emphases—as in "I wish now to wish now that it is now," where each *now* has a different syntactical use as well as emphasis—and by a kind of binding symmetry as in "And now how do you do now" and in "This which I think now is this." The rhetorical emphasis is sometimes thrown to the end of the line as a climax—as in "not now but now" and in "oh yes oh yes now"—or suspended as in the almost parenthetical "now that it is now"—or recovered for a fresh sequence and line by subordination—as in "that I will tell very well / What I think . . ."—or by question and answer, as in "What do I think now / I think . . ." Such variations of emphasis and balance, the changes of speed, the changes from statement to exclamation to question to answer to a question that is not a question but a greeting (how do you do)—all this does, once you have your eye on it, make an extremely eventful and vibrant stanza, culminating in the symmetrical, balanced, triumphant statement and conclusion "This which I think now is this."

I have made this rather minute analysis, which suspends
the live continuity of the poem and so is false to the essential,
in order to show that the poem, which looks at first childishly
simple and unorganized, is in fact a very varied and complex and
highly organized expression, out of the simplest elements of language and thought. The "beautiful disorder" *is*, rigorously, "an
effect of art." But her staying with such rudiments of thought,
word, and figure, making everything of them, living in their
sacredness and preciousness, when these are so often profane and
despised, is a natural result of that purity and tenderness and
all but religiosity of intention toward language which Sherwood
Anderson remarked in her long ago—especially toward "the little
housekeeping words, the swaggering bullying street-corner
words, the honest working, money saving words, and all the other
forgotten and neglected citizens of the sacred and half forgotten
city [*of words*]." So that when, as she said, she "completely
caressed and addressed a noun" in writing "A rose is a rose is a
rose is a rose," it was not a passing fancy but from the center of her
intention.

With the best will in the world, our sense of language is de-
bauched, as politics, advertising, the newspapers, and even conversation rarely spare it, so it may be difficult to focus on the
small essentials of the language or to see a full beauty in them;
and yet a reader who is really accustomed to modern poetry or to
say Gerard Manley Hopkins may have less trouble. Hopkins deals
in a richer musicality and a sumptuous imagery, but as a rhetori-
cian and, intellectually, as an *actualist* to the verge of heresy, he
is germane to the manner. His sense of the syllable, the monosyl-
lable and its placing, with its fullest meaning, and his sense of the
simplest and minutest grammatical and rhetorical figures, if
familiar to the reader at all, may help him with these "Stanzas," if
the "Stanzas" are unfamiliar.

Few of the "Stanzas" are as easy as the one I quoted, and only
the most intrepid reader should try to begin them at the beginning and read through consecutively. If read at random, as one
may read the Old Testament or *In Memoriam*, they yield more
more readily, or so they have to me. Another way of warming to
the work or of getting one's attention in focus, is to pick out the
one-line stanzas scattered through the work and get the hang of

them before trying the longer ones. For the sake of a little more
order and method in case of need, I offer this list of relatively
simple stanzas, though it should be strayed from:

Part II, 14, 18; Part III, 2, 10, 12; Part IV, 9, 24; Part V, 5, 13,
25, 29, 33, 41, 48, 51, 59, 60, 61, 63, 75.

No, they are better read at random, because one of the delights
of rambling about in them is encountering very fine aphorisms.
Here are a few I liked:

"In changing it inside out nobody is stout"—meaning nobody thrives by making the subjective objective. This could lead
directly to a dispute about the "objective correlative" as against
a subjective correlative, but it is meant to stand and not lead,
not even to the thought which succeeds it in the meditation.

"That which they like they knew"—meaning that what people like is what is already familiar. Here, explanation is otiose to
the point of fatuity, except that by contrast a paraphrase does
point up the solid elegance of Gertrude Stein's expression, the
fine ring of her new coinage of an old commonplace.

"There is no hope or use in all." This axiom is as pretty in
itself as Euclid's on the straight line, and its applications are many,
but in the "Stanzas" the natural application is to writing, and
there it is true enough, that a complete work or a complete
thought is an absolute in itself and contains no future, neither
hope nor use, and this may exalt you or horrify you, depending
on what you feel a piece of writing should be or do, on whether
you like thought as an end or as a means.

"What is strange is this." Or, it is immediate experience, not
the remote and imagined, which contains novelty and romance.
The sentence could stand as a motto for nearly all of Gertrude
Stein's work, or of Hopkins', or indeed for all philosophies of im-
manence or presence. One may disagree with such an aphorism,
as one may not agree that all things flow or that to be is to be
perceived, but one cannot resist the shapeliness of its utterance,
nor even deny that it covers its immense ground, indeed holds it.

The other long work in this volume, "Winning His Way," is
a narrative poem, written in 1931, the year before the "Stanzas,"

and is less concerned with *sense*. It is based rather on *sound*—on the musical and temporal elements of writing—and on what I have called absolute eventuality. Narrative poetry was not much of an issue in 1931, but eventuality as "narrative" did offer—as did *sense*—an extrication from *sight* then, and I believe it is an even more promising solution now, not so much from *sight* as from the current exasperation of *sense*.

One constant problem of narrative poetry is to keep clear of the versified novel, or short story, or drama, that is, to make the poem so essentially and energetically a poem that it carries the narrative element instead of being carried by it. I know of no great success with such a poem since Pushkin, for the later 19th century swamped the lyricity of its narrative in pictorial and novelistic developments. If there is to be a tradition behind what I am persuaded is the coming narrative poetry, it will have to be pre-Tennysonian and probably, to support a concentration and intensity proper to our times, rely on the medieval *lay* rather than the epic or even the ballad, which has a way of being a series of lyricible situations. I may easily be mistaken about all this, but even if the coming composition is to be more a matter of dispersion than of concentration and onward eventuality, the dispersion will surely be pyrotechnic rather than developmental as in the 19th century or the average epic. In any case, "Winning His Way" is interesting as opening possibilities of technique, in this perspective.

It professes to be "a narrative poem of poetry"—as reflexively as the "Stanzas" are discursive poems of or on poetry—but it does treat lyrically the bits of scenes, situations, events, and relationships that would make up a regular narrative. The "story," as a structure of consecutive happenings to be followed, has been pretty thoroughly destroyed by its explosion or transsubstantiation into lyricism, and the "narrative" is now almost entirely in the verbal and lyrical events of the poem itself, which moves at an astonishing pace. The movement seems to have surprised Gertrude Stein herself, for she announces quite early in the poem:

> And so. Now. A poem.
> Is in. Full swing.

And it goes on to a conclusion of Mozartean sweep and dash
—and with his perfect saturation of instant by instant eventuality.
For example, the device of sentences made of one or two or a
few more words is in part a simple brisk staccato but it also breaks
down the syntactical *structure* of the thought or statement into
a series of disjunct *events*. Where, in the "Stanzas," the line and
sentence do not progress but their series does, here progression
is induced into the line or sentence itself, making for much greater
and quicker movement, and a lyricity sustained in part on the
perpetually exclamatory sense. The exclamation is controlled of
course by the larger sense running through the sentences, and
varied considerably by the number of words to the sentence and
the number of sentences to the line. It is certainly a simple device,
but the range of effects and the variety of speed and movement
Gertrude Stein draws from it are extraordinary. Here is a fair
example—with a few bright remains of *sight* for heightening:

> It. Which. Is a suspicion. Of the. Imagination.
> They will part. But. Not partly.
> Because after all it is convincing.
> That he is great. And she is. Right.
> Let her eat. Plums and an apple.
> Let him. Eat. Currants and lettuce.
> Let them eat. Fish and bread.
> And all the other things. That make. Cake.
> Was theirs. Hers. A disturbance.
> He spoke reasonably. And authoritatively.
> And they. Will know. That.

Whether coming narrative poetry uses a consecutive story
or whether it uses, like this, fragments and aspects of a story as
the occasions for continuous lyrical events, the problem of making the lyrical movement, that is, the specifically poetic movement, dominate and control the inert lapse of regular narrative
time will still be an essential problem to narrative poetry, and
"Winning His Way" is very instructive in this regard, a tech-
nician's paradise. Besides which it is one of Gertrude Stein's hap-
piest works, where she is not so much struggling to create the
form as possessing it and playing it for all it is worth. If one ac-

cepts the terms of the game it makes delightful reading, not very difficult, and much lighter and slighter than the "Stanzas."

The remaining poems, the shorter ones, have charms and interests of their own, though I think some of them contain weary or perfunctory passages, like "A Poem" of 1933 and "Poems" of 1931—and even these have their good moments. But all of them are interesting as versions of or sketches for or relaxations from the two major performances, the "Stanzas" and "Winning His Way." "For-Get-Me-Not," of 1929, is an early exercise in the staccato style, a series of short lyrics, some of them of great beauty, like "Advice about Roses," but only a beginning toward the larger use of the method in "Winning His Way" and *A Wedding Bouquet*. "A French Rooster," "Abel," "Narrative," and "A Ballad" are all exercises in poetic narrative and in the interactive movement and balance of line, sentence, and stanza. Some of these still rely on the pastoral sweetness she had mastered in 1927, in *Lucy Church Amiably*, and on a brilliant, lavish, and tender use of color, but the severer and intenser forms are gradually becoming articulate. "To Help," of 1930, turns these accomplishments to a very gay and simple miniature drama, a predecessor of *A Wedding Bouquet*, "Short Sentences," and a good many other poetic dramas or plays, even operas, as this vein of experiment broadened.

"A Little Love of Life," of 1932, is a loose and lively discursive poem containing such lines as "Eat your apple darling" and no doubt a distraction from the rigors of the "Stanzas." So, no doubt, was "Margite Marguerite and Margherita," a discursive description, in much the same verse as the "Stanzas," of three women with not quite the same name and not quite the same character—a pretty elaboration of the fancy she had already exploited in the play "The Five Georges," that people with the same name resemble each other in character.

In 1932, after reaching the terrible attenuation of the "Stanzas" at their purest, she suddenly changed and, partly for distraction, wrote *The Autobiography of Alice B. Toklas*, concrete to the point of gossip, and as simple a narrative as anyone could ask, though in some of the purest prose of our time. Though many works were still to come, and many handsome exploits both in her popular style and in more difficult styles, she never, I think, returned to the problem of the "Stanzas." The forms she used for philosophical discourse were in many ways richer, with plays and images and parables, with a great variety of intellectual games, but none of them is quite the monumental attempt at absolute thought the "Stanzas" are. She left off abruptly but at the same time deliberately and with a curious acquisition of calm, a sort of rocklike wisdom. The poems called rightly enough "Afterwards" and "First Page," written in 1933, mark her departure and a new beginning. They are less intense, less vibrant, than the "Stanzas," but they have a very moving tranquillity. In "First Page" comes the passage:

> This which I say is this. One way of being here to-day.
> I simply wish to tell a story, I have said a great many things but the emotion is deeper when I saw them [*that is, when her writing was largely sight or "painting"*]. And soon there was no emotion at all and now I will always do what I do without any emotion which is just as well as there is not at all anything at all that is better.

Not that she did not return to emotion, for World War II brought out some of her most passionate and eloquent writing, but this lucid tranquillity remained at the heart of it, and gave her courage to face the dangers of the war, and afterwards to die as she chose. But all that belongs to her life, her legend, her writing. It is, as she would say, all there. And I think the "Stanzas" and "Winning His Way" are, rather, *here*, that it is at the point at which she left them that we come in.

CONTENTS

STANZAS IN MEDITATION (1932)

PART I

Stanza I

I caught a bird which made a ball
And they thought better of it.
But it is all of which they taught
That they were in a hurry yet
In a kind of a way they meant it best
That they should change in and on account
But they must not stare when they manage
Whatever they are occasionally liable to do
It is often easy to pursue them once in a while
And in a way there is no repose
They like it as well as they ever did
But it is very often just by the time
That they are able to separate
In which case in effect they could
Not only be very often present perfectly
In each way which ever they chose.
All of this never matters in authority
But this which they need as they are alike
Or in an especial case they will fulfill
Not only what they have at their instigation
Made for it as a decision in its entirety
Made that they minded as well as blinded
Lengthened for them welcome in repose
But which they open as a chance
But made it be perfectly their allowance
All which they antagonise as once for all
Kindly have it joined as they mind

Stanza II

It is not with them that they come
Or rather gather for it as not known

They could have pleasure as they change
Or leave it all for it as they can be
Not only left to them as restless
For which it is not only left and left alone
They will stop it as they like
Because they call it further mutinously
Coming as it did at one time only
For which they made it rather now
Coming as well as when they come and can
For which they like it always
Or rather best so when they can be alert
Not only needed in nodding
But not only not very nervous
As they will willingly pass when they are restless
Just as they like it called for them
All who have been left in their sense
All should boisterous make it an attachment
For which they will not like what there is
More than enough and they can be thought
Always alike and mind do they come
Or should they care which it would be strange.
Just as they thought away.
It is well known that they eat again
As much as any way which it can come
Liking it as they will
It is not only not an easy explanation
Once at a time they will
Nearly often after there is a pleasure
In liking it now
Who can be thought perilous in their account.
They have not known that they will be in thought
Just as rich now or not known
Coming through with this as their plan
Always in arises.
Liking it fairly and fairly well
Which meant they do
Mine often comes amiss
Or liking strife awhile

Often as evening is as light
As once for all
Think of how many often
And they like it here.

Stanza III

It is not now that they could answer
Yes and come how often
As often as it is the custom
To which they are accustom
Or whether accustomed like it
In their bought just as they all
Please then
What must they make as any difference
Not that it matters
That they have it to do
Not only for themselves but then as well
Coming for this.
He came early in the morning.
He thought they needed comfort
Which they did
And he gave them an assurance
That it would be all as well
As indeed were it
Not to have it needed at any time
Just as alike and like
It did make it a way
Of not only having more come
She refused to go
Not refused but really said
And do I have to go
Or do I go
Not any more than so
She is here when she is not better

When she is not better she is here
In their and on their account
All may remember three months longer
Or not at all or not in with it
Four leaf clovers make a Sunday
And that is gone

Stanza IV

Just when they ask their questions they will always go away
Or by this time with carefulness they must be meant to stay
For which they mind what they will need
Which is where none is left
They may do right for them in time but never with it lost
It is at most what they can mean by not at all for them
Or likeness in excellent ways of feeling that it is
Not only better than they miss for which they ask it more
Nearly what they can like at the best time
For which they need their devotion to be obtained
In liking what they can establish as their influence
All can be sold for which they have more seeds than theirs
All can be as completely added not only by themselves.
For which they do attack not only what they need
They must be always very ready to know.
That they have heard not only all but little.
In their account on their account can they
Why need they be so adequately known as much
For them to think it is in much accord
In no way do they cover that it can matter
That they will clear for them in their plight
Should they sustain outwardly no more than for their own
All like what all have told.
For him and to him to him for me.
It is as much for me that I met which
They can call it a regular following met before.

It will be never their own useless that they call
It is made that they change in once in a while.
While they can think did they all win or ever
Should it be made a pleasant arrangement yet
For them once in a while one two or gather well
For which they could like evening of it all.
Not at all tall not any one is tall
No not any one is tall and very likely
If it is that little less than medium sized is all
Like it or not they win they won they win
It is not only not a misdemeanor
But it is I that put a cloak on him
A cloak is a little coat make grey with black and white
And she likes capes oh very well she does.
She said she knew we were the two who could
Did we who did and were and not a sound
We learned we met we saw we conquered most
After all who makes any other small or tall
They will wish that they must be seen to come.
After at most she needs be kind to some
Just to like that.
Once every day there is a coming where cows are

Stanza V

Why can pansies be their aid or paths.
He said paths she had said paths
All like to do their best with half of the time
A sweeter sweetner come and come in time
Tell him what happened then only to go
Be nervous as you add only not only as they angry were
Be kind to half the time that they shall say
It is undoubtedly of them for them for every one any one
They thought quietly that Sunday any day she might
not come

In half a way of coming that they wish it
Let it be only known as please which they can underrate
They try once to destroy once to destroy as often
Better have it changed to progress now if the room smokes
Not only if it does but happens to happens to have the room
smoke all the time
In their way not in their way it can be all arranged
Not now we are waiting
I have read that they wish if land is there
Land is there if they wish land is there
Yes hardly if they wish land is there
It is no thought of enterprise there buying
Might they claim as well as reclaim.
Did she mean that she had nothing.
We say he and I that we do not cry
Because we have just seen him and called him back
He meant to go away
Once now I will tell all which they tell lightly.
How were we when we met.
All of which nobody not we know
But it is so. They cannot be allied
They can be close and chosen.
Once in a while they wait.
He likes it that there is no chance to misunderstand pansies.

Stanza VI

I have not heard from him but they ask more
If with all which they merit with as well
If it is not an ounce of which they measure
He has increased in weight by losing two
Namely they name as much.
Often they are obliged as it is by their way
Left more than they can add acknowledge
Come with the person that they do attach

They like neither best by them altogether
For which it is no virtue fortune all
Ours on account theirs with the best of all
Made it be in no sense other than exchange
By which they cause me to think the same
In finally alighting where they may have at one time
Made it best for themselves in their behalf.
Let me think well of a great many
But not express two so.
It is just neither why they like it
Because it is by them in as they like
They do not see for which they refuse names
Articles which they like and once they hope
Hope and hop can be as neatly known
Theirs in delight or rather can they not
Ever if shone guessing in which they have
All can be glory can be can be glory
For not as ladling marguerites out.
It is best to know their share.
Just why they joined for which they knelt
They can call that they were fortunate.
They can be after it is all given away.
They can. Have it in mine.
And so it is a better chance to come
With which they know theirs to undo
Getting it better more than once alike
For which fortune favors me.
It is the day when we remember two.
We two remember two two who are thin
Who are fat with glory too with two
With it with which I have thought twenty fair
If I name names if I name names with them,
I have not hesitated to ask a likely block
Of which they are attributed in all security
As not only why but also where they can
Not be unclouded just as yes to-day
They call peas beans and raspberries strawberries or two
They forget well and change it as a last

That they could like all that they ever get
As many fancies for which they have asked no one.
Might any one be what they liked before
Just can they come to be not only fastened
It should be should be just what they like
This day in unison
All out of cloud. Come hither. Neither
Aimless and with a pointedly rested displeasure
She can be glad to be either in their resigning
That they have this plan I remember.
Well welcome in fancy.
Or just need to better that they call
All have been known in name as call
They will call this day one for all
I know it can be shared by Tuesday
Gathered and gathered yes.
All who come will will come or come to be
Come to be coming that is in and see
See elegantly not without enjoin
See there there where there is no share
Shall we be there I wonder now

Stanza VII

Make a place made where they need land
It is a curious spot that they are alike
For them to have hold of which in need of plainly
Can be suddenly hot with and without these or either
For themselves they can change no one in any way
They can be often placid as they mean they can force it
Or wilder than without having thought Frank Wilder was
a name
They knew without a thought that they could tell not then
Not known they were known then that is to say although
They were just as famous as in when in eloquence shortly

Every one knowing this could know then of this pleased
She can be thought in when in which it is in mine a pleasure.
Now let me think when.
There should not be this use in uselessness.
It is easier to know better when they are quite young
Over five and under fourteen that they will be famous.
Famous for this and then in a little while which it is lost.
It is lost.
By the time that they can think to sing in mountains.
Or much of which or meadows or a sunset hush or rather
By this time they could which they could think as selfish.
No one can know one can now or able.
They may be thought to be with or to be without now.
And so it happens that at that time they knew
Or it happens that as at that time they knew
Which made pages no delight they will be felt not well
Not as ours hours are polite.
Or they think well or violent or weeding
Or maybe they be spared or if they can be wanted finishing
Or better not prepared.
It is not ordinary standing or standard or which.
Might they be mostly not be called renown.
Should they finish better with batches.
Or why are theirs alright.

Stanza VIII

I ought not to have known that they came well
Came here to want it to be given to them
As if as much as they were ever anxious to be not
Only having seen me they could be nearly all polite.
It was difficult to know how they felt then.
    Now I know everything of which it is that there is no
difference
    Between then and now but very much the same

As of course then it was not only here.
There they came well
Here they come well
Often make it be believed that they marry
It is not only that there was no doubt.
Indicated why they left in fear
Just as the same just is the same
They will be ought and autocratic
Come when they call.
They are called that they see this
They which is made in any violence
That they mean please forgive a mess
They can be often polite in languages.
Nobody thinks a thing.
They will welcome all shawled
I like a noon which has been well prepared
Well prepared never the less.
Hours of a tree growing. He said it injured walls.
We said the owner and the one then here preferred it.
Imagine what to say he changed his mind.
He said it would not matter until ten years or five.
She can be not unusual.
Or she can be taught most in exaggeration.
Or she can be moved once to balance all
Or she can be just unkind.
It is hoped that they feel as well
Oh yes it is hoped that they feel as well.
Argued with what they like or where they went.
Which they must have in any case
For accidentally they do not mean this.
Will there be any difference with how much they know
Or better than on account of which they much and wish
arranged
Can we call ours a whole.
Out from the whole wide world I chose thee
They can be as useful as necessity
More than they called which they could ask combined

Or made of welsh a treasure.
They mean me when they mean me

Stanza IX

With which they can be only made to brush
Brush it without a favor because they had called for it
She can be never playing to be settled
Or praying to be settled once and for all
To come again and to commence again or which
They will be frequently enjoyed
Which they never do as much as they know
That they like where they happen to have learnt
That seeds are tall and better rather than they will
It is much chosen.
Every year dahlias double or they froze

Stanza X

Might they remember that he did not dislike
Even if there was a reason that he did not choose
Nor rather as it happened which when he did not go away
They might which they not alone as nearly selfish
They will have placed in their own winning.
I know how much I would not have liked that.
They may be taken which is not the same as told
Made in which time they will frankly share
Might it be often not as well that they will change
Or in a way or principally in place
Made which they may which they made made unkind
It is not why they asked them would they like it

It is managed when they are able to agree
I come back to think well at once of most
Not only that I like it that they like it
But which in which way
That they chose
It is for instance not at all a necessity.
That once or twice or agreeable
Might they be very often very welcome
By which they mean will they come.
I have thought that the bird makes the same noise differently
Just as I said how will you do it if you like it
And they will not stretch well from here to there
If they know that in the full moon they should not plant it
Just before.
All might all mean that is the way to do
Not better than they have lost
But which they manage in their requital
I have known that sound and this as known
Which they will interlace with not only there
But the pale sky with the pale green leaves
Or which they will as they belong to trees
In this in their amount.
I come back to remember they will pay
Which they may do which they may say
Or which they may do whatever they do say
Always as often as they mention this
Which might annoy them does annoy them
As they call a pail a pail and make a mountain cover
Not only their clouds but their own authority
For having been here then as it is better to be
Which is an arrangement better made for them
Than not alone for them for which they will be wetting.
It came very closely but no one was just yet
Not to be frightened as they meant at all
I do not care that he should make threads so
Threads are tenderly heads are tenderly so and so
Very well merited
I should judge just inclined

Neither as disturbance or better yet
Might it be changed but once before
Left them to gather it wherever they can and will
Just the same.
It might be very well that lilies of the valley have a fragrance
And that they ripen soon
And that they are gathered in great abundance
And that they will not be refreshing but only
Very lovely with green leaves
Or managed just the same when payed or offered
Even if they do.
They will never be careless with their having stayed away.
I know just how they feel with hope
And their wishes after all will we come
No we will not come.
In any absent way we will not only not be there
But when will we be here in one way
Any mixing of which it is in their presence
They or renowned or will they be made there
Will they be made there could be a question
Any answer could not be a question to their arrangement.
After all if it came out it meant it came again
Of course any one always is an answer.
Once in a while one or two
They could count now with any obstruction
As much as they advance.
Will or well a price.
In looking up I have managed to see four things.

Stanza XI

But which it is not by that they are rich
But only for it not only when they may count
Or by the opening that they will go round
As having value for which they may plan more

In which they can attract a celebration
Of their own cause not only just as well as all absurd
Can they be well awakened because they have not heard
Or can they come to account as much as not abandon
By the time that they caused them not to blame
Just as much as they could as they fasten
Linking it not only as absurd but fairly often
Be they as well aware as not only not only fasten
But which they can wish as not only opening
Or very carelessly arrange by the time they will go
Finally not only why they try but which they try
In case of joining.
Why should nobody wait when they come there
They have met one who likes it by and by
He will learn more than it is often read
That they could always please
More than just by their count
After all why can they liken it to this
Or not only add very much more
Or not be any one known as politeness
It is not at all like or alike
An invitation suffices for the present
In the middle of their exchange
They can cease moderation
Or embellish no one at a time
But then to wonder if they will be more
Or if there will be more which follows by
They will be not at all leaving it
Any way do they differ as to excitement
Or stopping hastily with while in ambush.
They do delight that it was any bird
Made to be near than they could like to plan
Should be thought successor to their own
Without in pleasure may they like may now.
Just as soon as ever if they come
By that in trial that they manage
It is for this for which for them for her
Coming to think it only as they knew

Known makes it plain I shall
Think birds and ways and frogs and grass and now
That they call meadows more
I have seen what they knew.

Stanza XII

She was disappointed not alone or only
Not by what they wish but even by not which
Or should they silence in convincing
Made more than they stand for them with which
But they can be more alike than they find finely
In not only ordinary care but while they care
It is by no means why they arrange
All of which which they frustrate
Not only gleaning but if they lie down
One watching it not be left allowed to happen
Or in their often just the same as occasionally
They do not usually use that they might have mention
That often they are often there to happen.
Could call meditation often in their willing
Just why they can count how many are mistaken.
In not quite correctly not asking will they come.
It is now here that I have forgotten three.

Stanza XIII

She may count three little daisies very well
By multiplying to either six nine or fourteen
Or she can be well mentioned as twelve
Which they may like which they can like soon
Or more than ever which they wish as a button

Just as much as they arrange which they wish
Or they can attire where they need as which say
Can they call a hat or a hat a day
Made merry because it is so.

Stanza XIV

She need not be selfish but he can add
They like my way it is partly mine
In which case for them to foil or not please
Come which they can they can in June.
Not having all made plenty by their wish
In their array all which they plan
Should they be called covered by which
It is fortunately their stay that they can
In which and because it suits them to fan
Not only not with clover but with can it matter
That not only at a distance and with nearly
That they ran for which they will not only plan
But can be rain can be caught by the hills
Just as well as they can with what they have
And they can have it not only because of this
But because they can be here.
Or is it at all likely that they arrange what they like.
Nobody knows just why they are or are not anxious
While they sit and watch the horse which rests
Not because he is tired but because they are waiting
To say will they wait with them in their way
Only to say it relieves them that they go away
This is what they feel when they like it
Most of them do or which
It is very often their need not to be either
Just why they are after all made quickly faster
Just as they might do.
It is what they did say when they mentioned it

Or this.
It is very well to go up and down and look more
Than they could please that they see where
It is better that they are there

Stanza XV

Should they can be they might if they delight
In why they must see it be there not only necessarily
But which they might in which they might
For which they might delight if they look there
And they see there that they look there
To see it be there which it is if it is
Which may be where where it is
If they do not occasion it to be different
From what it is.
In one direction there is the sun and the moon
In the other direction there are cumulous clouds and the sky
In the other direction there is why
They look at what they see
They look very long while they talk along
And they can be said to see that at which they look
Whenever there is no chance of its not being warmer
Than if they wish which they were.
They see that they have what is there can there
Be there also what is to be there if they can care
They care for it of course they care for it.
Now only think three times roses green and blue
And vegetables and pumpkins and pansies too
She knew she grew all these through to you
And she can be there did he mind learning how now
All this cannot be mixed.
Once again I think I am reflecting
And they can be patient in not why now
And more than if which they are reflecting

That if they with which they will be near now
Or not at all in the same better
Not for which they will be all called
By which they will can be as much as if wishing
But which each one has seen each one
Not at all now
Nor if they like as if with them well or ordinarily
Should they be more enjoined of which they like
It is very well to have seen what they have seen
But which they will not only be alike.
They are very evenly tired with more of this
For they will happen to be in which resolve
Always made by which they prepare that no one
Is more able to be sure of which
They will not will they compel
Not only where they see which they see
But will they be willing for needing
Only which they could call not by it
If they have come again to do it not at all
As very much made in once by their own saying
Yes of course which they will not be at all
Not only not for them in which they like
I lead all may be caught by fattening
Or not either sent all which can positively say so
In their own pleasure neither which they like
It is mine when they need to accept add me
For which they mind one at a time
It is at one time no different between how many hills
And they look like that caught in I mean
For which they will add not when I look
Or they make it plain by their own time.
This which they see by
They turn not their back to the scenery
What does it amount to.
Not only with or better most and best
For I think well of meaning.
It is not only why they might stare to change
Or feel crops well as he has promised, he said.

That there would be several days not of rain
And there would then be plenty of good weather
Probably the crops would be good.
Alright they think in wishes
And some superstitions and some
Beginning and fortunately with places of ditches
And also formidably of which when
When they find the clouds white and the sky blue
The hills green and different in shape too
And the next to what followed when the other bird flew
And what he did when he dug out what he was told to
And which way they will differ if they tell them too
And what they do if they do not cover the vine too
They do it by hand and they carry it all too
Up the way they did still have it to do
And so they think well of well-wishers.
I have my well-wishers thank you.

PART II

Stanza I

Full well I know that she is there
Much as she will she can be there
But which I know which I know when
Which is my way to be there then
Which she will know as I know here
That it is now that it is there
That rain is there and it is here
That it is here that they are there
They have been here to leave it now
But how foolish to ask them if they like it
Most certainly they like it because they like what they have
But they might easily like something else
And very probably just as well they will have it
Which they like as they are very likely not to be

Reminded that it is more than ever necessary
That they should never be surprised at any one time
At just what they have been given by taking what they have
Which they are very careful not to add with
As they can easily indulge in the fragrance
Not only of which but by which they know
That they tell them so.

Stanza II

It is very often that they like to care
That they have it there that the window is open
If the fire which is lit and burning well
Is not open to the air.
Think well of that is open to the air
Not only which but also nearly patiently there
It is very often why they are nearly
Not only with but also with the natural wine
Of the country which does not impoverish
Not only that but healthily with which they mean
That they may be often with them long.
Think of anything that is said
How many times have they been in it
How will they like what they have
And will they invite you to partake of it
And if they offer you something and you accept
Will they give it to you and will it give you pleasure
And if after a while they give you more
Will you be pleased to have more
Which in a way is not even a question
Because after all they like it very much.
It is very often very strange
How hands smell of woods
And hair smells of tobacco
And leaves smell of tea and flowers
Also very strange that we are satisfied
Which may not be really more than generous
Or more than careful or more than most.
This always reminds me of will they win

Or must they go or must they be there
They may be often led to change.
He came and when he went he said he was coming
And they can not be more in agreement
Than cakes are virtuous and theirs is a pleasure
And so they either or a splendid as a chance
Not to be seen to be not impervious
Or which they were not often as a chance
To be plainly met not only as anxious.
Will they come here I wonder why
If not will they try if they wonder why
Or not at all favorably
Just as can as in a way
A cow is and little cows are
He said it so and they meant more
Which it is for this an occasion or not
Just as they please
Can they be just as careful as if they have a chance
To be not only without any trouble
Or can be they came

Stanza III

They can lightly send it away to say
That they will not change it if they can
Nor indeed by the time that it is made
They can indeed not be careful that they were thankful
That they should distinguish which and whenever
They were not unlikely to mean it more
Than enough not to decide that they would not
Or well indeed if it is not better
That they are not cautious if she is sleepy
And well prepared to be close to the fire
Where it is as if outside it did resemble
Or can be they will relinquish.
I think I know that they will send an answer.
It can be sensibly more than they could
That one sheep has one lamb and one sheep has two lambs
Or they can be caught as if when they had been

Not only as they like but she can say
He can say too two can be more that is to say
Three can be more than one more
And only after they have five nobody
Has quarreled not only for them but after a while
She knows that they know that they
Are not remarkable.
It is often more which they use that they
Knowing that there is a month to-day
In which often they use or can they use
Which they knew it could be in no venture
That they will use he will carefully await
And leave it like that to be carefully watching
Will we come and will we come then
They can to which can they be to which they use
Or not at all as in a fashion
More than kind.
It is often so that they will call them
Or can be there for which they will not see them
Nor can they us what they will like
In for instance will they change this for them.
Coming by themselves for them in no matter
Could one ask it is not usual
That if they are polite they are politer
Or either of them not to be one for them
Which they can call on their account for them.
It is all all of which they could be generous
If no one gave more to them
They could be with them all who are with them
For them can they be more than many
Not only but righteous and she would be
Not angry now not often for them
With not as told not by them
It is very well to have no thorough wishes
Wish well and they will call
That they were remarkable
And it is well to state that rain makes hills green
And the sky blue and the clouds dark

And the water water by them
As they will not like what they do not have
As nobody has been indifferent
Not only will she regret
But they will say one two three
Much as they use.
It is very well to know.
More than to know
What they make us of
Although it is cold in the evening
Even if a fire is burning and
Summer is of use to them

Stanza IV

All who have hoped to think of them or wonder
Or can be they will like what they have had
More than they should if they went away freshly
And were very modest about not knowing why it was
That they were not denied their pleasure then
For which they can be more than not inclined
Which makes it plainly that in one way it made no difference
That they were always said to be just when they came
There where they liked and they were not allowed
Not only ordinarily but just now
They were agreeable which is why they are they
They hesitate they more they come where they are standing
They will take courage which they will not want
Nor will they worry very much as why they wait
They will not be often there
Think well of how very agreeable it is to meet them
To say yes we will go we know where we have been
We will say yes it is not without trouble that we came
Nor do we manage definitely to share.
But we must with one and all go there.
It will be often fortunately that strawberries need straw
Or can they yes indeed have marsh grass ready
It will support all who will have support
And she will kindly share hers with them

His with them
More than that they will stop this for them
Not only certainly but very surely
No one needs kindly any disappointment
Will they step in and out and can easily
One heel be well and one heel one be well
Or as an ever ready change for once in a while
There can be reasons too why there are reasons why
If they can be said as much
That they will stay behind not only here but there
For them in a way they stay

Stanza V

Be careful that it is not their way not to like that
Not only not to be careful but to be very much obliged
Also moreover not to be the cause of their going
But which they will endeavor not to change
Not only for this but by the time
That which they knew there they must remain
If for them not at all it is not only why they like
But which they may wish from foolishness
Once at a glance.
It is not only why they are careful to replace
Not only which they can as they disturb
Or any weakness of wishing they would come there
More often than they do or carefully not at all
As it is their care to bestow it at one time
Should they because or in or influence
Not only called but very likely called a sneeze
From first to last by them in this way introduces
Them one at one time.
It is at once after that they will be better than theirs
All alike or all alike as well or rather better not
It can only not do not do all of which
They prefer elaborate to why they while away
Their time as they can accidentally manage
As a chance in which provocation is what they can call
Or while they went they gathered more

In made in gain
And more than all of it called cold
Or why they should arrange carefulness
Not only is our neat but as our plan
Named called useful as it is understood
Just why they could they interpose
Just fortunately in around about
At all managed getting ready there
To be determined but not by themselves alone
As often as they are more there
Which interested them.
They could be bought necessarily two or taken
In place of when they were attached to whatever
It is left to be planned that they can call
For it in all the hope that they can go
Or stay away whichever it is made to like
As they may mean or mean to do
It is fortunately by all of them
Made not only with this but for this.
A change from rest or a change from the rest
Well and welcome as the day which when the sun shines
Makes water grow or covers others more
Than when they looked there where they saw
All of which when they had not wondered
Would they like it there best
Might I ask were they disappointed.

Stanza VI

When they were helped as every one can
Once when they do and once when it is
Not only their feeling but also their way
Not to suppose that they will wish
That they can receive nor more than suggest
From which they look as much as if ever they can
That they will oblige which will be for them
Not only theirs but nearly as much
As theirs not alone but which they can
Not only join but nearly so

Make their arrangement believe their own way
Come whichever they can in whatever way
That they conclude that they must use
It not only for them but without any doubt
As they will hear better or not so well
In which and on which occasion
They will not only call but let them know
Not only what they allow but whatever they wish
As not only theirs.
It is a chance that they will be left
Or be consoled by each with one as no mistake
But they attach themselves they do trouble
They come when they will
They allow. They can establish.
They can even agree not only to what they have
But should they be more than bereft
If they not only see but not only see
All or more than all because and because
Of which they are obliged
Being as they are to go there.
It is very kind of them to come.
As well as they can because and moreover
When they think well they think without that
Which moreover makes it yield
Because it is an instance of often now
Not only with it but without it
As even when and once in a while
As much as they change theirs in their own
As once allowed because they undertake can
As they can positively learn
Which it is mine to have then.
All that they can do is theirs not only then
They can often be thought all as at once
More often they will relish
At once they can change it
It is not only if at once that they are all
Or do they like it too
Or can they see it all

Or even might they not like it
If it is at once whatever they claim.
It is not only not a misfortune
It is wholly theirs to be believe me

Stanza VII

What do I care or how do I know
Which they prepare for them
Or more than they like which they continue
Or they can go there but which they mind
Because of often without care that they increase aloud
Or for them fortunately they manage this
But not only what they like but who they like.
There can be said to be all history in this.
They can be often opposite to not knowing him
Or they can be open to any impression
Or even if they are not often worried
They can be just bothered
By wondering do they often make it be alike afterward
Or to continue afterward as if they came
It is useless to introduce two words between one
And so they must conceal where they run
For they can claim nothing
Nor are they willing to change which they have
Oh yes I organise this. But not a victory
They will spend or spell space
For which they have no share
And so to succeed following.
This is what there is to say.
Once up a time they meant to go together
They were foolish not to think well of themselves
Which they did not were they willing
As they often were to go around
When they were asked as they were well aware
That they could think well of them
Remember this once they knew that the way to give
Was to go more than they went
For which they meant immediately faster

It is always what they will out loud
Can they like me oh can they like me.
No one can know who can like me.
This is their hope in wishing however
When they were not only laden with best wishes
But indeed not inclined for them to be careless
Might they be often more than ever especially
Made to be thought carelessly a vacation
That they will like this less.
Let me listen to me and not to them
Can I be very well and happy
Can I be whichever they can thrive
Or just can they not.
They do not think not only only
But always with prefer
And therefore I like what is mine
For which not only willing but willingly
Because which it matters.
They find it one in union.
In union there is strength

Stanza VIII

She can be thought to be accurate with acacia
Or by and by accustomed to be fairly
Just why they should in often as in or often
Could they call a partly necessary for them
Or why should anxiousness be anxiousness
Or their like that because more than they could
They will be named what do they do if the like
Or could they be troubled by it as a thought
Should they consider that they will gain
By not having it made for them to join
They will plainly state that only then only only there
More than if they will show all of it
Because please be plain for this time
And do not couple that they abandoned
Or which they abandoned because not only they
were not used

In better than whenever or wherever they will go
I think I do not sympathise with him.
It is often known how they are just how they are
And if they are often just as well as being here
It is not at all unlikely they will change
And this you know all of it which you know
Be only thought not to please.
I think that if I were faithful or as bought
Or should be checked or as thought
Or finally they can claim for it more
Or just why they are identified
Or pleading they will call it all they know
Or have it that they make it do
Not only as they have not only as they have
It is other than theirs that they think is worth while
But which they come frequently to separate
In advantageous or advantage by their time
That they will come at once or not
For which they will come way of nine
She may be thought better have it spared them
That they will cover other than allowance.
He will come to show well enough all there
Or better have it strange or come again
Night like or night like do.
It is very foolish to hesitate between do and dew.
Or not at all broadly on which account
They can favor or fulfill or never marry
It is while while they smell that all it came
It came to be very heavy with perfume
Just like it can only it was not more than just
Why they went back.
Back and forth.
I have often thought it to be just as well
Not to go only why not if they are going
But they will like why the look
They look for them and they are reminded.
That often any day all day
They will not go alike but keep it.

However much they say.
How many did you know
Or not say no.
Or no
Come to couple spelling with telling.

Stanza IX

Just why they could not ask them to come here
Or may they press them to relieve delight
Should they be planned or can they cause them then
To have it only lost they do not care to leave
Should they come when and will they forward it back
Or neither when they care just when they change
Can they not leave or will they not allow
More than they wish it is often that it is a disappointment
To find white turkeys white and little ones the same
Should they be pleased or should they rather not be pleased
Or more than they do should they rather keep it for them
Or more than this should they not infrequently
Or now when they see the difference between round
and about
Or not only why they change but what they change
One for one another.
It is often a very best need that they have
To come to see that after all
It was after all when they came back
Or need they not be provoked
By thinking that they will manage to please them.
How often very often do they go
Not which they wish or not which they wish
However it is better not to like it at all
I find it suddenly very warm and this can easily be
Because after all may be it is
In which case do they need any more explanation
Or indeed will they bother
Or after all can there be any difference
Between once in a while and very often
And not at all and why not and will they

Should they be pleased with everything just the same
So that they will think how well they like
What they will do which they do
For them at all.
It is often no matter and a difference
That they see this when they look here
And they can very well be ready
To see this when they look where they do
Nor or can they be there where they are
But not there where they are when
They are at once pleased with what they have
As they do not wish not only but also
To have it better where they like.
It is often no purpose not to have disgrace
Said that they will wait.
All often change all of it so.
It may be decided or not at all
That it is meant should they use
Or would they care to, think well long
Of what they think well.
And thank you
It is why they ask everything of them.
Should it be equally well planned
Made to carry or please it for them too
As they can often care or the difference
Between care and carry and recall
Should they find it theirs can they
Will they not be thought well of them.
Or not at all differently at once.
She can have no illusions
Nor be prepared not to be baffled
Or think well of them for which awhile
They chose.
It is for this that they come there and stay.
Should it be well done or should it be well done
Or can they be very likely or not at all
Not only known but well known.
I often think I would like this for that

Or not as likely
Not only this they do
But for which not for which for which
This they do.
Should it be mine as pause it is mine
That should be satisfying

Stanza X

It is not which they knew when they could tell
Not all of it of which they would know more
Not where they could be left to have it do
Just what they liked as they might say
The one that comes and says
Who will have which she knew
They could think all of which they knew as full
Not only of which they could they had as a delight
Or could it be occasionally just when they liked
It was not only theirs that they used as this
Not which they had with them not with them told
All have it not in any way in any anger
But they have it placed just when not there
For which they will allow could it or would it be told
That they shall not waste it to say to them
All of which after a while it is
As an arrangement
Not only theirs and only not at all.
They must be always careful to just be with them
Or they will not only not be but could be thought
To change which they will never know
Not only only all alike
But they will will be careful
It is not only this that antagonises that
Or they may be just as well in their refreshment
They will do always they will always do this
They could not relieve often which they do
They could be thought will it do
Once more come together does it matter
That it could be that they showed them this

But not this that they showed them that they showed
them that
 Or only once or not with not as only not once
 Could they come where they were
 Not only so much but also this much
 Just whenever they liked this much
 Which they were to declare
 That no one had had corroboration
 For which they will not only like
 Letting once make it spell which they do
 They can call it not be it as careless
 Not only to ask but neither rested for
 Which they will better can it have it
 Not only there around but this
 It is pleasantly felt for all
 Not only why they liked with which
 They came for it with their undertaking
 Made that they will or use or will they use
 By which they will know more than they incline
 Coming as it does coming as it does
 Are they allowed
 After all if it is so

Stanza XI

I thought how could I very well think that
But which they were a choice that now they know
For which they could be always there and asking
But made not more than which than they can like
Not only why they came but which they knew
For their own sake by the time that it is there
They should be always rather liking it
To have not any one exclaim at last
It must be always just what they have done
By which they know they can feel more than so
As theirs they can recognise for which they place
And more and moreover which they do
It is not only to have all of it as more
Which they can piece and better more than which

They may remain all or in part
Some can think once and find it once
Others for which for which they will
It is at no time that they joined
For which they joined as only
Not for which it is in partly measure
Having alike be once more obtained
They made no trouble as they come again
All which they could
But they will care
All for which it is at once thought
Just when they can surprise
No one in what they could there
Make without any pause a rest.
They will think why they
And they will come
In response.
Should they be well enough.
Otherwise they can consider that
Whatever they have missed.
I think I know I like I mean to do
For which they could they will place
He will place there where
It is finally thought out best
No means no means in inquietude
Just when they give and claim a reward
Not for which they go and get this
They have been with the place their place
Why is there not why is there not with doubt.
Not able to be with mine.

Stanza XII

One fortunate with roses is fortunate with two
And she will be so nearly right
That they think it is right
That she is now well aware
That they would have been named
Had not their labels been taken away

To make room for placing there
The more it needs if not only it needs more so
Than which they came

Stanza XIII

But it was only which was all the same

Stanza XIV

It is not only early that they make no mistake
A nightingale and a robin.
Or rather that which can which
Can which he which they can choose which
They know or not like that
They make this be once or not alike
Not by this time only when they like
To have been very much absorbed.
And so they find it so
And so they are
There
There which is not only here but here as well as there.
They like whatever I like.

Stanza XV

It is very much like it.

Stanza XVI

Could I think will they think that they will
Or can they be standing as seated still
For which they will leave it make it be still
That they will reach it for which they will until
They should be said to be planned for which they will
Not which they need not plan not more than will
It is an estimate of ferocity which they would not know
Not with surprise nor from the wish
That they would come at all
Can they be mentioned
For which they can not be only lost
For which they will can they can they come in

For which they will not but very likely
But they can not be there with which they will
For they can be with that kind that is what is
When they can like it as they do
But which they can not be for them
All made as they are not without it
Often left to them to come to arrange this
More than they can at most.
It was not only that they liked it
It is very kind of them to like it.

Stanza XVII

Come which they are alike
For which they do consider her
Make it that they will not belie
For which they will call it all
Make them be after not at least ready
Should they be settled strangely
Coming when they like an allowance
Naming it that they change more for them
With which which is certainly why they waited
They can be more regularly advised
In their case they will be able
Not only which they know but why they know
It is often that do their best
Not only as it is but which in change
They can be as readily which it is alike
Theirs as they better leave
All which they like at once
Which nearly often leave
This is the time in which to have it fasten
That they like all they like
More than which they can redeem.
It is often very well to if they prey
Should they could should they
They will not be imagined fairer
If they next from then on
Have it as not diminished

They can place aisle to exile
And not nearly there
Once in a while they stammer but stand still
In as well as exchange.
Once in a while very likely.
It is often their choice to feel it
As they could if they left it all
A ball fall.
Not two will give
Not one will give one two
Which they can add to change.
They will change what they like
Just what they do.
One two three or two

Stanza XVIII

She can be kind to all
If she wishes chickens to share
Her love and care
But they will think well of this
Which can not be amiss
If they like.
Two dogs for one or some one.
It is a happy wish
For some one.

Stanza XIX

She can think the thought that they will wish
And they will hold that they will spell anguish
And they will not be thought perverse
If they angle and the will for which they wish as verse
And so may be they can be asked
That they will answer this.
Let me see let me go let me be not only determined
But for which they will mind
That they are often as inclined
To have them add more than they could
She will be certainly seen if not as much

They will be left to be determined
As much as if they pleased they pleased
Not only theirs but only theirs
For them as much as known and not only
Not repeated because they will be seen
Partly and for less for which they are not very clearly
Made to be better than often as serviceable
Is it as much as why they like
For which they are often as much mistaken
Anything astonishes a mother or any other.
A stanza in between shows restlessly that any queen
Any not a stanza in between for which before which
Any stanza for which in between
They will be for which in between
Any stanza in between as like and they are likely
To have no use in cherishing.
They could be not alone consoled
They could be they can can they
Finally relieve.
It is often eight that they relinquish a stanza
Just when they feel that they are nearly
That they can could and do color
For which they will not only be inconvenient
For which they all for a forest
Come in as soon as our allowed
They prepare nor do they double
Or do they add prefer to before and call
She can be ours in allusion not only to
But why they will as much encourage
Readily for instance or can for instance
Come with not only as much as they tell
They tell it because if not why not
Such should be called their glory or their make
Of angling with and for around
Can it be wading for which they wade
Theirs once again the same
All which they said it said it in and answered
May be they like

Might it be uncontained likely
That they should as much joined with ease
But not by this for once once is not only one
They presume once alike not by their own present.
They present well. It followed once more
Only theirs in case. For which.
They add conditionally to not previously adding
More than they gave to one.
One is not one for one but two
Two two three one and any one.
Why they out tired Byron.

PART III

Stanza I

For which can they it which
That they can then or there either
By means of it for which they could
Recognise it is more than in going
They can come will they come until
The exactingly which they in exact
For which they will in and
They need not be for which they go
Theirs is all but not which it is in a chance
That they could incline to be inclined
For them or not or more inclined
Now not at all deserting
Nor not at all deserting
For which they finish English
Can they make cake or better
For which when did he like
Theirs or not at all theirs
They will not leave a well alone
Or not because now the water comes
Just as they could.

They are always just not even
He is at least tired by the heat
Or he will
Just not join not just join
All that they like to do.
It is why I see when I look out at it
That it is just like when I see it
And it is fortunately not a bit of it
By this for which they please come out
Of there.
Can they call one forty might
Or it is not might it
If it is not only they did
But which will they if they do
Not only this or which but can or can
Should more not any more
Any day make raspberries ripe
As they can do make what they do there
In leaving having had which
Not only while they do not but while they do
In often not at all now I am sure
Not sure not only how
But can it be at once.
Now to suppose it was like that.
Every time he went he went
And so it was not that they went
Not not at all.
And when he came back not when he went
He came back not when he came back
When he went.
One not to come to go when not to be
Not only not from here not here from there
Just as they used as usual
For which it it is not that that it
Must not do go
They leave it there is no there they do do
They do not do one two
As all round any arranged is not in at best

Once they he did once he they did or not
At all at any time.
It is so much that there is no difference in so much.
One one and two two one.

Stanza II

I think very well of Susan but I do not know her name
I think very well of Ellen but which is not the same
I think very well of Paul I tell him not to do so
I think very well of Francis Charles but do I do so
I think very well of Thomas but I do not not do so
I think very well of not very well of William
I think very well of any very well of him
I think very well of him.
It is remarkable how quickly they learn
But if they learn and it is very remarkable how quickly
they learn
It makes not only but by and by
And they can not only be not here
But not there
Which after all makes no difference
After all this does not make any does not make any difference
I add added it to it.
I could rather be rather be here.

Stanza II

It was not which they knew
But they think will it be though
The like of which they drew
Through.
It which may be that it is they did
For which they will be never be killed
By which they knew
And yet it is strange when they say
Who.
And so not only not here
May be they will be not in their place there
For which they will what will they may be there

For them for which not only very much
As is what they like there.
Now three things beside.
Add which not which to which
They wish which they divide.
If a fisherman fishes
Or else a well
Very well does an attack
Look back.
For that in use an extra make a moment
Further in use which they can be there when
In open use of which they like each one
Where they have been to have been come from.
It is often that they do regularly not having been
Before.
As much as and alike and because
Once before always before afraid in a dog fight
But not now.
Not at all now not when they not only wish to do
Can they be ours and very pretty too.
And you.
Once more I think about a lake for her
I do not think about a lake for them
And I can be not only there not in the rain
But when it is with them this it is soon seen
So much comes so many come.
Comfortably if they like what they come.
From.
Tables of tables and frames of frames.
For which they ask many permissions.
I do know that now I do know why they went
When they came
To be
And interested to be which name.
Who comes to easily not know
How many days they do know
Or whether better either and or
Before.

She can be eight in wishes
I said the difference is complicated
And she said yes is it it is
Or she said it is is it.
There seems so much to do
With one or two with six not seven
Either or.
Or believe.
That not only red at night can deceive.
Might they we hope better things of this.
Or of this.
Is.
When they are once or twice and deceive.
But leave
She can be called either or or before
Not only with but also with
With which they wish this
That they will like to give rain for rain
Or not.
It is just like it sounds.
I could not like it then nor now
Out now
Remained to how.
However they are careful.
Having forgotten it for them
Just how much they like
All potatoes are even when they have flowers
All adding is even
If they asked them
Would they ask them.
It would not be like alike for which
They did.
They had and did.
But which they had which they had which they is and did.
Gotten and gotten a row
Not to in did not and in said so
It is not only that I have not described
A lake in trees only there are no trees

Just not there where they do not like not having these
Trees.
It is a lake so and so or oh
Which if it is could it does it for it
Not make any do or do or it
By this it is a chance inclined.
They did not come from there to stay they were hired
They will originally will do
It is not only mine but also
They will three often do it.
Not now.
Do I mind
Went one.
I wish to remain to remember that stanzas go on

Stanza III

Not while they do better than adjust it
It can feeling a door before and to let
Not to be with it now not for or
Should they ask it to be let
Can they be sent as yet
For can they can they need met
Way and away in adding regret to set
And he looks at all for his ball.
I thought that I could think that they
Would either rather more which can
For this is and antedated a door can be
Which after all they change.
He would look in the way
Of looking.
Now added in again.
It is a way having asked in when
Should they come to be not only not adding some.
I think it is all very well to do without that
But it is why they could be with without that
For which they called a time
Not having finished to say that nearly there
They would be neither there as box wood grows

And so if it were they could be as easily found
As if they were bound.
Very nearly as much a there
That is one thing not to be made anything
For that but just for that they will add evening to anything

Stanza IV

Not which they know for which they like
They must be last to be not at it only with
It can for which they could with an a
Many can not come in this for nor without them
Some of which will they for them awhile
For which it is not only at an attempt
They can find that they can retouch
Not only what should be cared for
So they make this seem theirs
And only integrally shared as much as fine
They will out and out confer
That they will always can be so
As what they like.
Be mine prepared
What can it be not for their add it to
Can and delight for which not why they neglect
Just when or just when
For which not more than
Or by nearly
It is not their coat.
They must care for their furniture
Not but as one
For could and forfeit too
Coming and one.
It is not only that they could be here
When they are often made just can
It is my own that no one adds for it
Not only is it added well
She can only cloud go around
By that in awoken
Could and clad

Can they be eaten glad
Should not only should not under known
Say any way
A way
Equal to any stanzas are all three
They must be spared to share
Should it not only this and all around
They will have will appointed
Not only why they look not that
They call meadows are or all
For it is not only only their name
But which is a plain and a plain plaintive
Too or more.
I can not be indifferent to a little while
By which all tall at all
They could be not only any in any case
What does he mean by that
Not only not only not any interest not interested
But they will a valley.
Once every day they ate to a day
Not obliging not at not to obliging
But she will have meant
Or they will but they maintain
Ease by a minute.
It is not only their four in amount
Or while or a while
Or going
Or just as soon by which ought
Will they not have any as presence
They could be ought they be manage
Not only she thinks which
Just as never which many which
Made or manage they thrust.
It is often all they order or in order
But which they endanger
Do or not do.
However can be in account of whatever they do.

Stanza V

It is not a range of a mountain
Of average of a range of a average mountain
Nor can they of which of which of arrange
To have been not which they which
Can add a mountain to this.
Upper an add it then maintain
That if they were busy so to speak
Add it to and
It not only why they could not add ask
Or when just when more each other
There is no each other as they like
They add why then emerge an add in
It is of absolutely no importance how often they add it.

Stanza VI

By which are which add which a mounting
They need a leaf to leave a settling
They do not place a rein for resting
They do not all doubt can be a call
They can do which when ever they name
Their little hope of not knowing it.
Their little hope of not knowing it.

Stanza VII

By it by which by it
As not which not which by it
For it it is in an accessible with it
But which will but which will not it
Come to be not made not made one of it
By that all can tell all call for in it
That they can better call add
Can in add none add it.
It is not why she asked that anger
In an anger can they be frightened
Because for it they will be which in not

Not now.
Who only is not now.
I can look at a landscape without describing it.

Stanza VIII

That is why a like in it with it
Which they gay which they gay
But not only just the same.
Now who are now
Our who are now
It is not first not they are
But being touching all the same
Not and neither or the name.
It is very anxious not to know the name of them
But they know not theirs but mine.
Not theirs but mine.

Stanza IX

Tell me darling tell me true
Am I all the world to you
And the world of what does it consist
Can they be a chance to can they be desist
This come to a difference in confusion
Or do they measure this with resist with
Not more which.
Than a conclusion.
Can they come with can they in with
For which they can need needing
It is often by the time that not only
Which waiting as an considerable
And not only is it in importance
That they could for an instance
Of made not engaged in rebound
They could indeed care
For which they can not only
Be very often rested in as much
Would they count when they do
Is which which when they do

Making it do.
For this all made because of near
No name is nearly here
Gathering it.
Or gathering it.
Might it in no way be a ruse
For it which in it they an obligation
Fell nearly well.

Stanza X

Now Howard now.
Only righteous in a double day
It is ought frown
They could however collaborate
As only in the way
Of not only not renowned.
What is it often
Oh what is it often
Or should
Should as any little while.
Think more what they mean
Oh think more what they mean
Now I know why he said so
Oh no.
It is if it is.
What is the difference.
What is the difference both between for it and it
And also more also before not it.
It can be an absence better than not before.
It is just why they tried.

Stanza XI

I only know a daisy date for me
Which is in wishes can forget for it
Not which not that that is
And is that that not be that with
It is not any one can think
Why be without any one one can

Be favored flavored not which
It is not only not only neither without
But this is only so.
I cannot often be without my name.
Not at all
They will not wonder which at a time
And can it be alright.
They can lead any one away.
Now look not at that.
Having heard now hearing it
Should just engage those
Not always connected
Readily express
For them forget
It is very easy to be afraid to hear one come in.
All like all to go
There is often when they do not mention running
Or walking or not going
Or not why they do not find it in for him.
Just why they should or just why
Ate or bate or better or not sigh
He she can sigh and try why
They seize sigh or my.
It is often when it is not stated
That at it two or to
That it is better added stated
That they are to
I often like it not before
They do not or do not listen one to one another
Or by guess.
It is just as much as allowed
Why they carry or
All would or wood or wooden
Or all owed
Or not vestiges or very sight
Of water owned or own
Or not well velvet
Or not aligned

Or all or gone
Or capitally
Or do or comforting
Or not
Renown.
They will say pages of ages.
I like anything I do
Stanza two.

Stanza XII

Stanza ten make a hen
Stanza third make a bird
Stanza white make a dog
Stanza first make it heard
That I will not not only go there
But here

Stanza XIII

In changing it inside out nobody is stout
In changing it for them nobody went
In not changing it then.
They will gradually lengthen
It.

Stanza XIV

I could carry no one in between

Stanza XV

Can thinking will or well or now a well.
Wells are not used any more now
It is not only just why this is much
That not one can add it to adding main
For never or to never.
Suppose I add I like to
I can should show choose go or not any more not so
This is how any one could be in no hope
Of which no hope they did or did not
There is no difference between having in or not only not this

Could it be thought did would
By it a name.
I think I could say what nobody thought
Nobody thought I went there
This is however that they add sufficiently
Because it is not better allowed
All will come too.
Just joined how to houses
But they will like an only name
They could be thought why they had a weakness
To be sure.
Now this is only how they thought.
Let no one leave leaves here.
Leaves are useful and to be sure
Who can or could be can be sure
I could think add one add one advantage
That is how they like it.

Stanza XVI

She does not who does not it does not like it
Our our guess yes
But it does not it does not who does guess it
But they will place it or not place it yes
They could in insistence have nobody blamed
Which they do ours on account
Can they or can they can they blame this
This that they will wail when not in resting
But which they for which they could date and wait
Will they do what they are careful to do too
Or like this will they like this where they go
When it is not only not certain where they went
they were here
At all as likely as not up and down up and down to go
Not because before by which they attracted
They were with an on account which they knew
This not only not which they need blessing
Which or not which when they do not or which way
They do go

It is not inadvertent that they oblige
It is waiting they gather what do they like
Cherries not only not better not ripe
It was a mistake not to make not only a mistake with this
In not only in all noon after noon that they like
It is always arbitrary to come with bliss
For them to join it to come with it
They could manage just what they did
But did they not feel that
They could be not only not allowed but not clouded
It was very different again
Just when they join that they look.
They refer to a little that is a little trunk
A very little trunk once.
How very sorry they are for not for placing
Well place well
Just once to join and not too alike
That they go
Or will they not only in place of which to happen to be last
not to save it to say so
Or go.
And so they went carefully together.
As they like it which
They mean that for when
It is not mine
Fine

Stanza XVI

It is not which they will not like or leave it as a wish which
they compare
All of most all for that did they if not as it is
Should they dare or compare
Could it have been found all round
Or would they take pleasure in this
Or can they not be often whichever
As they told theirs in any day.
Does it make any difference if they ask
Or indeed does it make any difference

If they ask.
Would they be different if nobody added it all
Or looking just alike do they mind any extra
Can they or should they combine
Or should they not easily feel
That if they could they can or should
We ask.
Be not only without in any of their sense
Careful
Or should they grow careless with remonstrance
Or be careful just as easily not at all
As when they felt.
They could or would would they grow always
By which not only as more as they like.
They cannot please conceal
Nor need they find need they a wish
They could in either case they could in either case
Not by only for a considerable use.
Now let only it be once when they went
It is of no importance to please most
One of them as it is as it is now
It is not only for which they cause
That it is not only not why they like
Them.
They could often be a relish if it had not been thought
That they should write.
They will be only not more a choice
For which alone they remain.
Proclaim.
I wondered why they mentioned what they like.
All of which only what they knew
Just why they yearn
Or not rest more.
A counter and not a counterpane
They could be relished.
Just why they called wait wait.
What is it when there is a chance
Why should they like whatever they do

Not only if they will but if they will
Not only
It is not more than this shame.
Shame should not be for fountains.
Not even not yet.
But just when the mountains are covered
And yet they will please of course they will please
You which it is.
Not any not on any account
Can it not only be why they want.
It is always which they like.
It is a thought give a thought to Cuba
She could in cooking
And only not let owls frighten not birds
Not only not
Because in only ending birds
Who ends birds where.
Now I have said it.
It is of no use one year
A toad one year
A bird a little very little as little bird one year
And if one year
Not only not at all one year.
It came very difficultly.
Just not in not in not in not as in him.
And so on account on account of reproach.
Could they if not she would be startled.
But they cost neither here nor there.
Just as I think.
Once when they should they if indifferently would
When to look again
Pinny Pinny pop in show give me a pin and I'll let you know
If a pin is precious so is more.
And if a floor is precious so is not a door.
A door is not bought twice.
I do think so earnestly of what.
She had no chagrin in beauty
Nor in delight nor in settled sweetness

Nor in silkiness alright.
But why often does she say yes as they can say
She finds that if one is careful one has to be very much
Awake to what they do all need.
Now often I think again of any english.
English is his name sir.
That much is not only not only not a disadvantage
Over them.
Once more I wish italian had been wiser.
But will they wish
They wish to help.
And their wish succeeded.
And added.
Once more I return to why I went.
I went often and I was not mistaken.
And why was I not mistaken
Because I went often.

Stanza XVII

Not only this one now

Stanza XVIII

How can no one be very nearly or just then
Obliged to manage that they need this now
She will commence in search not only of their account
But also on their account as arranged in this way
She will begin she will state
She will not elucidate but as late
She will employ she will place adding
Not with it without it with their account
Supposing they can say the land stretches
Or also can be they will say it is all told
Or perhaps also they will say
Or perhaps also they will say that they went from
here to there
Or not only just then but when just then
Also perhaps not only might they not try
Can be not only what they wish but will they wish

Perhaps after a while it is not why they went
Not only which it is but after it is
They might be thought to have it not known
Only which they are obliged
To feel it at all not which they can know
They could call colors all or not
Incomplete roses.
They find fish an ornament
And not at all jealously at any and all resemblance
They have been warned to try and be called all
For which they plan a favor
Should they be thought to be caught all around
By that time it is well to think it all
Not only can they be
It is a pleasure that twice is neglected
In which amount.
They anticipate in place.
Could no one try of fancies.
However how is it if it is right and left.
Or rather should it did it happen to be more
They can allowed or stranger
They have not then once cost
But which in theirs and on which occasion
Can they be minded.
Now how can I think softly of safety
Which which they do
It is not only their only hindrance
But not well won not with it.
In intermittence can they remind sees.
She can fortunately not count
If she says but which if they say
But which they find.
Now only this when they all think.
How can she manage our places.
It is for this they could recall
Better than all do.
It was not often that I could not join them
Which they did.

Now how could you disguise joins
By which it is in ate and dishes
They could be only they could be only worried
By what they remain with what they will
Or not unkind.
This is what I think I think I often did the same
When they should be all there as known
After all I am known
Alone
And she calls it their pair.
They could be cut at noon
Even in the rain they cut the hay
Hay and straw are not synonymous
Or even useful with them
Or even useful with them
Or as a hope that they did
Which after all they did not.
In this way any one or did add not a precaution.
Think how well they differ caution and precaution
Or not.
Or should they allow ours in a glass
For them they carry
Better not be strange in walking
They do or do not walk as they walk as they part.
Will they mean mine or not theirs
They will they will like what they entitle
Should they be theirs.
He asked did they that is it
That is did it mean it was with them
There with them
They could not be ought not be in mind
So then
All of which reminds no one
Having said.
Do which or they can be kind.
She says some or summer could be.
Not only not again for when.
I can think exactly how I found that out.

Just when they say or do
Once and before.
It is not only that they like
In the meantime.
If even stanzas do.

Stanza XIX

Not what they do with not
Not only will they wish what
What they do with what they like
But they will also very well state
Not only which they prefer by themselves
And now add it in aging ingenuity
And which they will as soon as ever they can
But which they tell indeed can they or can they not proudly
Not only theirs in eight but which they meant
They will all old declare
That believing it as a patent pleasure in their care
Nor where where will they go older than not
Nor will they furnish not only which they had but when
they went
In reason.
It is often that they allow a cloud to be white
Or not only patently white but also just as green
Not only theirs in pleasure but theirs in case
Not only however but not only however
Or not at all in wishes that they had chickens
Which can be alternately well or ducks
Or will they spread for them alone
Go be not only their care.
This which and whatever I think
I not only do but make it be my care
To endanger no one by hearing how often I place
Theirs not only why they are best not
Not by it as they like.
I have thought while I was awakening
That I might address them
And then I thought not at all

Not while I am feeling that I will give it to them
For them
Not at all only in collision not at all only in mistaken
But which will not at all.
I thought that I would welcome
And so I could be seen.
I then thought would I think one and welcome
Or would I not.
I then concluded that I might be deceived
And it was a white butterfly
Which flew not only not but also
The white dog which ran
And they they were accomplished
And once in a while I would rather gather
Mushrooms even than roses if they were edible
Or at least what not.
I do not wish to say what I think
I concluded I would not name those.
Very often I could feel that a change in cares
Is a change in chairs and not only can and cares
But places
I felt that I could welcome in anticipation wishes
Not only which they do but where they do
How are our changes.
When they could fix titles or affix titles.
When this you see hear clearly what you hear.
Now just like that not just like that
Or they will enjoin and endanger
Damage or delight but which they crow
They have threatened us with crowing
Oh yes not yet.
I cannot think with indifference
Nor will they not want me
Do will they add but which is not
Where they could add would or they would or not
For which they for which fortunately
Make it be mine.
I have often thought of make it be mine.

Now I ask any one to hear me.
This is what I say.
A poem is torn in two
And a broom grows as well
And which came first
Grows as well or a broom
Of course any one can know which of two
This makes it no accident to be taught
And either taught and either fight or fought
Or either not either which either
Can they be either one not one only alone.
Should it be thought gracious to be a dish
Of little only as they might mean curiously
That we heard them too
And this I mean by this I mean.
When I thought this morning to keep them so they
will not tell
How many which went well
Not as a conclusion to anxious
Anxious to please not only why but when
So then anxious to mean. I will not now

Stanza XX

Now I recount how I felt when I dwelt upon it.
I meant all of it to be not rather yes I went
It is not that now they do not care that I do
But which one will
They can not be thought nervous if they are left alone
Now then I will think of which went swimming.
It does make a difference how often they go
Or will they prepare that I know
I know this I know that I shall say so
Or can they choose an anagram
This one said this one.
If one we hurried for this one
Just when they did wish that it should be settled then
They could think let us go
Just when they will they can

All my dear or but which they can
Having been long ago not knowing what I felt
And now
It does make a difference that well enough a cow
Can be recognised now so then
If not twenty as ten
Or one enough without it then.
This that I can
I repeat I do not know what I felt then
Which they do which they do
Nor will they track it if they follow then
How are it is to do
A kite is a delight this I can do then
But not with then for which they allow them
This is the way not to end but to see when the beginning.
I like a moth in love and months
But they will always say the same thing when
They sing singing
I wish I could repeat as new just what they do
Or alike as they hear when they do not listen to every one
So she said it they but which they
She said the nest was empty but not so
The nest was empty that is to say not there
It was as if she looked alike
By which no one mean startled
Like that
I think I will begin and say everything not something
But not again and only again alike
Thank you for the touch of which they leave
He easily destroys my interest in may be they do
but I doubt it
But not at all with which by nearly which time
But just as well heard
Why should he not say he did say that
And it was amusing.
And by and by not which they do
I now I do not know what I feel
So in extra inclusion.

What do I think when I feel.
I feel I feel they feel they feel which they feel
And so borrowed or closed they will they will win
How can any one know the difference between
worry and win.
This is not the only time they think which they know
Or better not alright.
How can they eager either or and mend
She can mend it not very well between.
Of course he knows at what he does not only hear
Oblige me. I also oblige him. And think then.
Do I repeat I do not know what I do not see to feel which
they hear
Oh yes

Stanza XXI

When she meant they sent or a grievance
Was she meant that he went or a need of it henceforward
Was it with it that they meant that he sent or he thought
That they should not plainly have not bought
Or which they went to be naturally there
It is a pause in mistaken.
They could know that they would call
Or they would prefer it to before
On their account.
I should look if I saw
But she would send if she would intend to prefer
That they might cause it best and most.
It is not only which they go but when they go
Or if not said to send or say so
Now think how palpably it is known
That all she knows which when she goes
They look for him in place of that
Of which they are used or to be used
In preference
And so they halt more to partly do
Do or due or only dew or did you do it.
I could not favor leaves of trees to in any case

Place me to mine.
This is not what they care or for poetry.

PART IV

Stanza I

Who should she would or would be he
Now think of the difference of not yet.
It was I could not know
That any day or either so that they were
Not more than if they could which they made be
It is like this
I never knew which they can date when they say
Hurry not hurry I could not only not do it
But they prepare.
Let me think how many times I wished it.
It flattered me it flattered me it flattered me
And I was all prepared which they sent
Not only not why but where if they did not enjoy
Their place where they meant with them
And so they can be fitly retired.
This is what I saw when they went with them.
I could have been interested not only in what they said but in
what I said.
I was interested not interested in what I said only in what
I said.
I say this I change this I change this and this.
Who hated who hated what.
What was it that announced they will not mind it.
I do think often that they will remember me.
Now who remembers whom what not a room
No not a room.
And who did prepare which which vegetable very well
And might I not only feel it to be right to leave them to say
Yes any day it is because after which way

They shell peas and of the pea shell they make a soup to eat
and drink
    And they might not amount to calls upon them.
    They were in place of only where they went
    Nobody notices need I be not there only
    But which they send it.
    Not to think but to think that they thought well of them.
    Here I only know that pumpkins and peas do not grow
    Well in wet weather.
    And they think kindly of places as well as people.
    I should think it makes no difference
    That so few people are me.
    That is to say in each generation there are so few geniuses
    And why should I be one which I am
    This is one way of saying how do you do
    There is this difference
    I forgive you everything and there is nothing to forgive.
    No one will pardon an indication of an interruption
    Nor will they be kindly meant will be too or as a sound.
    I am interested not only in what I hear but as if
    They would hear
    Or she can be plainly anxious.
    How are ours not now or not as kind.
    They could be plainly as she is anxious
    Or for their however they do
    Just as well and just as well not at all
    How can you slowly be dulled reading it.
    It is not which they went for there were dishes
    It is not why they were here not with their wishes
    Or accidentally on account of clover
    I never manage to hammer but I did
    In with all investigation
    And now I now I now have a brow
    Or call it wet as wet as it is by and by
    I feel very likely that they met with it
    Which in no way troubles them
    Or is it like to.
    It did it a great deal of good to rub it

Stanza II

I come back to think everything of one
One and one
Or not which they were won
I won.
They will be called I win I won
Nor which they call not which one or one
I won.
I will be winning I won.
Nor not which one won for this is one.
I will not think one and one remember not.
Not I won I won to win win I one won
And so they declare or they declare
To declare I declare I declare I win I won one
I win in which way they manage they manage to win I won
In I one won in which I win which won I won
And so they might come to a stanza three
One or two or one two or one or two or one
Or one two three all out but one two three
One of one two three or three of one two and one

Stanza III

Secretly they met again
All which is changed in made they can be merry
For which they could in any regulation
Manage which they can have in any case a trial
Of when they do or sing sisters
And so much is taken for granted
In which appointment they color me
Or leave it as not in a glass or on the grass
They pass.
Not at all
For which no one is met in winning
They will be very well pleased with how they stand
Or which or to which or whither they repair
To change it to change it fairly
Or can they like all that they have

Let us think well of which is theirs.
Why do they not count
Count how do you count
There is no counting on that account
Because if there is which is not what I say
I will make it do any day to-day
Or not why
They allow me to apply for it
The call will they call by which they plan
I will not gain gain easier easily
One which one which not now.
Why do they like which they like or why not
It is often many or as much which they have seen
Seen is often very well said
I think I have no wish that they will come
With their welcome
Nor which they try not to do
In any case for which they formerly
Were not repaid.
They are readily not here.
Once more no one not one begins
This is the difference
Not it or argument
But which and when
They enfold not in unfold
Beware aware deny declare
Or and as much in told
They cannot be thought restless when they do come and go
Either one either say so.
I say I felt like that.
Once they came twice they went which one will do
Or which they like for them or will they do
What they ask them to do
I manage to think twice about everything
Why will they like me as they do
Or not as they do
Why will they praise me as they do
Or praise me not not as they do

Why will they like me and I like what they do
Why will they disturb me to disturb not me as they do
Why will they have me for mine and do they
Why will I be mine or which can they
For which can they leave it
Or is it not
I have thought or will they let
Them know the difference if they tell them so
Between let us not be reckless or restless
Or by word of mouth
Can they please theirs fairly for me.
Just why they lay with the land up.
Coming to see it so.
It was not once when they went away that they came to stay.
Why should all which they add be each
Each is a peach
Why can they be different and try to beside
Be all as all as lost
They do not hide in which way
Better call it mine.
Our ours in or made between alike
With which cakes bake cakes
And it makes cake or cakes polite
But if they all call not when they do
Who ought they try to be alike
Which or for which which they can do too.
I refuse I I refuse or do
I do I do I refer to refuse
Or what what do I do
This is just how they like what they send
Or how to refuse what is that
That they need to sound sound lend
Can you question the difference between lend.
Or not lend
Or not send
Or not leant
Or not sent
But neither is a neighbor.

A neighbor to be here
She can be he can be useful or not useful
When they did not come why did they not come here.
Believe me it is not for pleasure that I do it
Not only for pleasure for pleasure in it that I do it.
I feel the necessity to do it
Partly from need
Partly from pride
And partly from ambition.
And all of it which is why
I literally try not only not why
But why I try to do it and not to do it.
But if it well-known it is well-known

Stanza IV

Mama loves you best because you are Spanish
Mama loves you best because you are Spanish
Spanish or which or a day.
But whether or which or is languish
Which or which is not Spanish
Which or which not a way
They will be manage or Spanish
They will be which or which manage
Which will they or which to say
That they will which which they manage
They need they plead they will indeed
Refer to which which they will need
Which is which is not Spanish
Fifty which vanish which which is not Spanish.

Stanza V

I think very well of my way.

Stanza VI

May be I do but I doubt it.

Stanza VII

Can be can be men.

Stanza VIII

A weight a hate a plate or a date
They will cause me to be one of three
Which they can or can be
Can be I do but do I doubt it
Can be how about it
I will not can be I do but I doubt it.
Can be will can be.

Stanza IX

How nine
Nine is not mine
Mine is not nine
Ten is not nine
Mine is not ten
Nor when
Nor which one then
Can be not then
Not only mine for ten
But any ten for which one then
I am not nine
Can be mine
Mine one at a time
Not one from nine
Nor eight at one time
For which they can be mine.
Mine is one time
As much as they know they like
I like it too to be one of one two
One two or one or two
One and one
One mine
Not one mine
And so they ask me what do I do
Can they but if they too
One is mine too
Which is one for you
Can be they like me

I like it for which they can
Not pay but say
She is not mine with not
But will they rather
Oh yes not rather not
In won in one in mine in three
In one two three
All out but me.
I find I like what I have
Very much.

Stanza X

That is why I begin as much

Stanza XI

Oh yes they do.
It comes to this I wish I knew
Why water is not made of waters
Which from which they well
Can they be kind if they are so inclined.
This leads me to want to wonder about which they do
I feel that they shall be spared this
They will agree for which they know
They do not do or describe
Their own use of which they are not tried
Or most or mostly named to be where
They will not as willingly not declare
That they appeal but do not prefer a share
Of plainly when they will
It is this I wish any minute
Oh yes I wish do I I do wish any minute
For them for fortune or forlorn or well
Well what do you do either what do you do
But like it or not
This that they can think just think
She has put her hair up with hairpins
Or do or do not only just do not only think
Finally than this.

It might be worth any cost to be lost.
They like that which they did
He did he remembered not only that he did
Oh why should any one repine one at a time.
Curiously.
This one which they think I think alone
Two follow
I think when they think
Two think I think I think they will be too
Two and one make two for you
And so they need a share of happiness
How are ours about to be one two or not three.
This that I think is this.
It is natural to think in numerals
If you do not mean to think
Or think or leave or bless or guess
Not either no or yes once.
This is how hours stand still
Or they will believe it less
For it is not a distress yes
Which they can free to build
Not by a house but by a picture of a house
But no distress to guess.
For this they are reconciled.
I wish that they were known.
This which they permit they please.
Please can they not delight and reconcile
Could anybody continue to be
Made openly one to see
That it is very pleasant to have been
With them
When this you see.
Once when they were very busy
They went with me.
I feel that it is no trouble
To tell them what to do
Nor either is it at all a trouble
To wish that they would do what I do.

This is well and welcome to mean
I mean I mean.
Think however they will be ready
To believe me.
Think well of me when this you see.
I have begun by thinking that it is mine
It is mine many often one at a time
In rhyme.
Of course in rhyme which is often mine
In time one at one time
And so I wish they knew I knew
Two and one is two.
This is any day one for you.
This which I explain is where any one will remain
Because I am always what I knew
Oh yes or no or so
Once when they went to stay
Not which not only once or twice yesterday.
This introduces a new thought as is taught.
I wish I exchanged will they exchange me
Not at all.
This is why they bought a ball.
To give it to them to be all
All which they keep and lose if they choose.
Think how can you be and beware
And constantly take care
And not remember love and shove
By design.
It is well to be well and be well and be welcome
Of course not to made to be
Honorably four to three which they do.
This is how they think well of believing all of theirs
To have been known.
It is singular that they can not only succeed
But be successful.
How should they not speedily try
If they could or could not know
That I did it.

Which is why they are so quiet with applause
Or can be the cause
Of their waiting there
For their meal
If they had it.
It is very beautiful to be eight and late.
Why should any one be ready too
As well as not for and with you
Which they do.
See how one thing can mean another.
Not another one no not any not another one.
Or not any means not or can not might three to one.
That is what they say to play.
And which is white if they might
They will call that they spoke to her

Stanza XII

Just why they mean or if they mean
Once more they mean to be not only not seen
But why this beside why they died
And for which they wish a pleasure.

Stanza XIII

But which it is fresh as much
As when they were willing to have it not only
But also famous as they went
Not to complain but to name
This understanding confined on their account
Which in the midst of can and at bay
Which they could be for it as once in a while
Please can they come there.
This is an autobiography in two instances.

Stanza XIV

When she came she knew it not only
Not by name but where they came with them.
She knew that they would be while they went.
And let us think.

She knew that she could know
That a genius was a genius
Because just so she could know
She did know three or so
So she says and what she says
No one can deny or try
What if she says.
Many can be unkind but welcome to be kind
Which they agree to agree to follow behind.
Her here.
Not clearly not as no mistake
Those who are not mistaken can make no mistake.
This is her autobiography one of two
But which it is no one which it is can know
Although there is no need
To waste seed because it will not do
To keep it though perhaps it is as well
Not to belie a change of when they care
They mean I like it if she will do it
But they could not complain again.
Let me remember now when I read it through
Just what it is that we will do for you.
This is how they asked in a minute when
They had changed a pencil for a pen
Just as I did.
Often of course they were not welcomed there
When they meant to give it all they liked
Made many more beside beside
Which when they tried or cried
He could not have his way
Or care to please please
And prepare to share wealth and honors
Which if they or if they or if they
Had not had mine too.
More can they gain or complain
Of which announce pronounce a name
When they call this they feel
Or not at all a heel she changed all that

For them fair or at once they will change hair
For there or at once more than all at once
Whenever they can.
This makes no allowance
Now this is how they managed to be late or not.
When once in a while they saw angrily
Or impatiently yesterday
Or beguiling February
They could so easily be thought to feel
That they would count or place all or kneel
For which they had been frightened not to do
They felt the same.
In which on no account might they have tried
To be remained to try why
Shall they be careful at all or not.
This is why they like me if they think they do
Or not which they the time they care I care
Or when where will they name me.
However tried however not or cried
She will be me when this you see.
And steadily or whether will they compel
Which is what I tell now.
This is a beginning of how they went at once
When I came there cannot they compare
No they cannot compare nor share
Not at all not in iniquity much which they engage
As once in a while perfectly.
All many so or say
But this or which they can
Believe me I say so.
I have not said I could not change my mind if I tried.
More than just once they were there.
All this is to be for me.

Stanza XV

I have thought that I would not mind if they came
But I do.
I also thought that it made no difference if they came
But it does

I also was willing to be found that I was here
Which I am
I am not only destined by not destined to doubt
Which I do.
Leave me to tell exactly well that which I tell.
This is what is known.
I felt well and now I do too
That they could not wish to do
What they could do if
They were not only there where they were to care
If they did as they said
Which I meant I could engage to have
Not only am I mine in time
Of course when all is said.
May be I do but I doubt it.
This is how it should begin
If one were to announce it as begun
One and one.
Let any little one be right.
At least to move.

Stanza XVI

Should they call me what they call me
When they come to call on me
And should I be satisfied with all three
When all three are with me
Or should I say can they stay
Or will they stay with me
On no account must they cry out
About which one went where they went
In time to stay away may be they do
But I doubt it
As they were very much able to stay there.
However can they go if they say so.

Stanza XVII

How I wish I were able to say what I think
In the meantime I can not doubt
Round about because I have found out

Just how loudly difficulty they do
They will they care they place
Or they do allow or do not bow now.
For which they claim no claim.
It is however that they find
That I mind
What they do when they do or when they do not do
It.
It is not only not kind not to mind
But I do do it.
This is how they say I share I care
I care for which share.
Any share is my share as any share is my share
Of course not not only not.
Of course I do which I of course do.
Once I said of course often
And now I say not of course often
It is not necessary any more.

Stanza XVIII

She asked could I be taught to be allowed
And I said yes oh yes I had forgotten him
And she said does any or do any change
And if not I said when could they count.
And they can be not only all of three
But she can establish their feeling for entertainment
She can also cause them to bless yes
Or can be or can they be not
Made to amount to more than can they.
This is what they do when they say can they
It is often that it is by this that they wish this
When they will value where they went when they did
They will also allow that they could account for it
Or might they not only not choose
It is often whichever they were fortunate and not fortunate
To be for which they can in all they like
This is what they use
I have thought I have been not only like this

Or they can please or not please
Which for instance and forsaken and beside which
They will oh please they will
Not only when they can as if allowed
It is all of it which they knew they did.
This is what I say two to belie
One to date and decry and no one to care
And she made as rashly careful as not
When they could think twice just the same.
This is at any time when they do not often see them
Theirs when they went away
Not only not included but why not included
Only they will not agree to permanence
Not more than twice as much.
Very much as they say aloud
Will you be back in a minute or not.
Let me think carefully not think carefully enough
By which I mean that they will not please them so
Not even if they know that they went too
So it is gracious once gracious to be well as well
As when they like liked it.
This is what it is made to be able
To need whichever they could be well-furnished
All the same three now.
This could if it could lead it if it did
To a cow. Think of it.
This is what I return to say
If I never do nor I ever do
How can it be so if it is true
Or just true as through or you
Made which they like as much.
Now commence again to be used to their
Saying that their cousin was one
Who felt that it was not a name
To which they meant to think well of them.
This is however how they do not deny
That they will not try to care
To leave it there from time to time

At once
It is very well-known that they are indifferent not to wishes.
Can she be sought out.
I wish to say that any case of a failure
Is what they were spared.
I wish to think that they will place
Much as more than they wish
As their changing it not only for them.
Could any one influence any one
One and one.
Or not.
If not why not.
Or if not would they not be more than
If they were changing which way any one
In which way any one would not need one
If not one and one.
Or not by them.
It is made why they do if they call them.
They could recognise the sun if there was another one
Or not at all by me
When this you see.
Or not in an exchange there might
Be only why they should.
Be this as it might
She could be pleased to
Be not only with them but by them
As well as for them
Which makes it at a meaning
And their equal to delight and plight.
Which of which one.
I had many things to think about quite often
They will call me to say I am displeased to-day
Which they can in adding often.
It is not why they knew that it is
Not only why they went but if they went when they went.
By this time they are as often with us
But we think of leaving them with others.

We wonder about it.
And they will not know if we go.

Stanza XIX

I could go on with this.

Stanza XX

Should however they be satisfied to address me
For which they know they like.
Or not by which they know that they are fortunate
To have been thought to which they do they might
Or in delight that they manage less
For which they call it all.
This is what I say fortunately
I think I will welcome very well in a minute
There nicely know for which they take
That it is mine alone which can mean
I am surely which they can suggest
Not told alone but can as is alone
Made as likely for which no matter
As more than which is lost
Recommend me to sit still.
As more often they could not see him
Have it to be or not as not
It not made it not not having it
Should they fancy worshipping
Worshipping me is what they easily can
If they come to think still that they think it still
Just why not if not
I have changed forty-nine for fifty
And can she be meant.
Or would it be a nuisance to like no one
Or better not if not only not to change
Change it should stop with not
Do you feel how often they do go
Go and so and which and met and if
And they are riding

There are so many things to ride.
And water and butter
And can they be no chief to me
I am not only not chiefly but only
Not with care.
And so much as they ever think
Remain to remain and not remain if not remain mine.
I have abused not leaving it not following it out
I also have not which can they not which they plan.
All of which is in why they used
To use me and I use them for this.
This too we too or not to go.
I often think do they sound alike
Who hates that or a hat not I.
Now I will readily say not I
But which they read to ready
Or say not I can day or say
Not blindly for caution or which or what
What about.
This is how I however remain
Retain is considered whatever they gain
I gain if in the main they make plain
Just what I maintain if I use a fruit.
Should just when this be any chance.
Better why often.
I have thought why she went and if she went he went.
No one knows the use of him and her
And might they be often just tried
Can they mean then fiercely
Should it chance to cover them not enough
I mean a hat or head
And also what a chair
And beside what beside pride
And all at once tried to believe me
Coming as if it could be entitled
One which they won.
One two.
I often think one two as one and one.

One one she counted one one and this made
Economy not only which but of which
They will not kneel of which they do.
I could be just as well obliged.
Finally I move from which
You can deduce the sun shone
By this time
Out loud
All of which can be able to be
Do I make a mistake
And if I do do you not at all either or
This time it should not have followed
Or not either to do it.
Little by little they engage not to change
Or different as it is they might if they should
But they will manage to indifferently relieve
More of which they could alight and aloud.
It is very foolish to know that they might alight
Not only do.
This which they feel they must discourage
And everything I say.
I will tell how once in a while

Stanza XXI

I know that twenty-seven had been had
For which they know no name
But our equality can indubitably spell well
For it or for which or for might it be
That it is a change to think well
Of not only when but might they be just where
They will care
Now fancy how I need you.
I have thought which they meant as willing
It is often a disappointment to dispense without
They will cool not which but very most
Well as welcome without.
She said she knew what I meant too
He too.

Although although allowed out loud.
As if they could remember where there
And there where.
Should she join robust or not
Or fortunately for it as they are not without
It is easily eaten hot and lukewarm and cold
But not without it.
Could it be thought that I could once be here
Which if they will can they not
I have heard it well enough to know
That he has not only not been mistaken yet again.
While will they now.
Oh yes while will they now
You should never be pleased with anything
If so they will crowd
But if they crowd or yes if they crowd
Which is it which if they can seat them.
I often feel well when I am seated seating them or not so
I go to remain to walk and what
Always when when is it.
It is often however they are bright.
She could often say however they can say
You always have to remember say and not so.
It is always not only not foolish
To think how birds spell and do not spell well
And how could it do birds and words
I often say so not at all amount.
All who should think season did not mean what
What is it.
I have been and have been amounted to it.
When they come in and come in and out.
Naturally it is not.
Or however not a difference between like and liked.

Stanza XXII

I should not know why they said so.

Stanza XXIII

I cannot hope again if they could mean which they liked.

Stanza XXIV

It is easy to grow ours more.
Or for which they will need a place to be
They could thank if not think that they arrange
In a way would they be angry in a way
If they could more which when they gather peas
They feel that it is not right to pay
Nor which if they nor which if they stay there.
Who need share stay there with stay away
Who will decline publicly
What is it if they will wish
Or be for which they beguile when they wish
Or can be not for which they can be spoken
It does not bother me to not delight them
They should fancy or approve fancy
They could call or can they for which will they might
But not only be the time but if which they manage.
It is in partly a reason that they feel well
Nor might they be more enclosed.
Fortunately they feel that it is right
To not give it giving it
As they do them for curls.
It is not often that they are always right
It is not often that they are always right
But which aggression or a guess
Or please addition or please a question.
Or please or please or please
Or and a foil of near and place and which nature
Will they plan to fit it to not in a point.
I wish no one the difference between a point and place
Oh yes you do oh do you.
This which I do or for intend to know
They could or call or if it is a place
In this place the sun which is not all
Is not so warm as told if it is not cold
But very warm which if favorably it is.
I could if I knew refuse to do it.
Or just when they feel like it they try

Beside which if they surround my home
They come to stay and leave it as they like
Not only not because.
Wish if vegetables need the sun
Or wish if not only not the sun but none
Also wish if they wish that they will size alike
And only if which if a wish which they will oblige
Not only necessary but they think it best.
This which I reflect is what they like to do
They like me to do
Or but or well or do be well to do
For them to like to do if I like what I do
Enormously.
Fancy what you please you need not tell me so
I wish to go or if I do I wish to go
I have often been interested in how they forget to go
Also I have been interested in if they wish to go
I have been better able to determine.
Not only however but whichever they would like
If it were partly told
That she Madame Roux is never yet quite through
But which cannot annoy because I like to try
To see why will she be here
It makes a change in faces
Her face always can change seen near or far
Or not at all or partly far.
It is not partly as they can share
Why should it be like whom.
I think I know the share
Share and share alike is alone
And not when in integrally in a way.
She could often be made sympathetic in a way a day.
It might however be she seen to be all
They feel more than they could
In point of sympathy of expression.
Now when I should think of them of this.
He comes again they come in she can come to come in.
All this is why they like but remember that for me

I am to tell not only well but very well
Why I shall easily be for all to me.
This is the reason.
I have been not only not forgetting but not only.
They will call it a chance.
Because of this can be because of this.
Which not only be how do you like not only not be
They will be satisfied to be satisfactory
Now not only not but will it be their appointment
To come when they said they would.
I said I would tell
Very well what is it that they plan to carry
Of course they plan to carry
How should it be better to put not any blue but that
Not any blue but that and change the mind
The ear and always any obligation.
Once more think twice of that.
It is very difficult to plan to write four pages.
Four pages depend upon how many more you use.
You must be careful not to be wasteful.
That is one way of advancing being wasteful
It uses up the pages two at a time for four
And if they come to and fro and pass the door
They do so.
This is my idea of how they play
Play what play which or say they plan to play which
Which is in union with whichever
They could be thought to be caught
Or planned next to next nearly next to one time
At one time it was very favorably considered
That they would oblige them to go anywhere.
Remember how we could not disturb them
It is very important not to disturb him
It is also important to remember this
Not if they disturb him
But really will they disturb him
I often do I not often think it is time to follow to begin
They could establish eight or arrange

This is not why they please or add as carelessly
They will have no use for what they said.
Now I wish all possibly to be in their shuddering
As to why if they came in and out
If they came in and out
What is the use of union between this with this.
They will add any word at most.
If she said very much or little or not at all
If she said very much or not at all
If she said a little very much or not at all
Who is winning why the answer of course is she is.
When I say that I know all of the might she be mine
She is it is particularly to care
To make it do she offers it as a compromise
To have been needed about I have not only
Not changed my mind.
Now let us think not carelessly
Not all about not allowed to change or mind.
Mind what you say.
I say I will not be careful if I do
I also say I should say what I do
I also do have a place in any antedated rose.
A rose which grows. Will they like that.
She will like that.
We have decided that only one dahlia is beautiful
That salads are not necessary
And that she has been very kind about pansies.
How can you change your mind.
This is what they know as collection.
A collection is why they place it here.
I often think how celebrated I am.
It is difficult not to think how celebrated I am.
And if I think how celebrated I am
They know who know that I am new
That is I knew I know how celebrated I am
And after all it astonishes even me.

PART V

Stanza I

If I liked what it is to choose and choose
It would be did it matter if they chose and choose
But they must consider that they mean which they can
If to-day if they find that it went every day to stay
And what next.
What is it when they wonder if they know
That it means that they are careful if they do what they show
And needless and needless if they like
That they care to be meant
Not only why they wonder whether they went
And so they might in no time manage to change
For which which fortune they went or meant
Not only why they like when they sent
What they mean to love meant.
It is this why they know what they like.
I like to have been remembered as to remember
That it meant that they thought when they were alike
As if they meant which they will undergo to choose
In which they can remain as little as they claim
In which not is it you
But which it is it is not without you
That they knew you and so forth.
This can be mine at night
Which does it mean to care.
Not only why they liked but just as if they liked
Not only what they meant but why they will not.
This is what there is not or yet.
Not to continue to do their best yet.
Think however I came to know it all.
I often offer them the ball at all
This which they like when this I say
Can they be called to play once in a way of weight

Or either our roses or their cake
I wish I had not mentioned which
It is that they could consider as their part.
Now then I had forgotten how then
Nor made it please away a weight
Oh yes you like it
Or if not for what if now and then
Without them it is often meant to be mine.
Let me say how they changed apart alike.

Stanza II

If you knew how do you very well I thank you
Or if you knew how do you do how do you
Or if not that changes more to many
And may be they do or not if not why.
This is how it is that it does not make any difference
To please them or not or not
Or not to not please them or oh yes yes.
They could should they under any circumstance
Understand differ or differs.
It is why they wondered if they liked
What indeed makes no difference
As they manage
To relieve plunders and blunders
Any one is often thought susceptible.
Or which one wishes.
Now I have wandered very far.
From my own fireside.
But which they knew in a wonder.
It is a wonder that they like it.
-I have often thought that she meant what I said.
Or how do you this about that.
Or if at any time.
It had been not only not remembered
I depend upon him I depend upon them.
Of or how they like.
This what I say makes me remember that.
That if it did

Which can just as you said
Or which can be
If they managed it
Or by the time they did.
This is however just how many are alike.
Once upon a time who will be left to rain
Or like it as much as ever
Or even more than that if they like it.
They must be often thought to be just as careful
As not to give them give anything away.
However how many do like to.
This is not what I meant by what I said.
It should be that I think that it might do
If I made it do
I also think that I should not say
That they know which way
They could arrange to go and say
That they will not stay if not
If not what do they like alike
Or as much as just yet.
I could often be caught liking it
Oh yes I could
And then it can not only if they say so.
Oh yes only not yes.
In just this way they went as they can
I have refused went and went as much.
I also have refused whatever they went.
But if wherever they went.
Not one in any two
Or just arise or if not only not to like.
It can not be alright.
When they thought how often about a wall.
When they thought how often about a wall.

Stanza III

Just when they wish wish
Or will they or must they be selfish
To not do you should not do not do

Not as if not to to to do
There that is better.

Stanza IV

I like any two numbers more than any two numbers before
Or not.
But if it had been alright to be bright.
Could I have been bright before or not.
I wonder if I could have been bright before or not
Not only why they do but if they do what I like
If I do what I like.
I could not nor can I remember
Whether if they were there if they were there to care
May be they could be wondering if it were like
If it were like it as it is
As it is if they meant only which
Whenever it is by this time
Of course no difference makes no difference at all.
I wish to think about everything anything if I do.
Or by the time easily
Or not only why they should.
Or please believe.
That they mean what they mean by that.
If not why should no one mind what they say.

Stanza V

Please believe that I remember just what to do
Oh please believe that I remember just what to do
Or please believe that I do remember just what to do
And if I remember just what to do
There will not only be that reason but others
Which at one time.
I like what I have not prepared before of course not.
As fast as not so fast
Not that it does not make any difference.
This is what they like what I say.

Stanza VI

This one will be just as long
As let it be no mistake to know
That in any case they like what they do
If I do what I do I do too
That is to say this conclusion is not with which.
It can be just as well known
Do you change about mutton and onions or not.
This is why they sleep with a ball in the mouth
If not what is there to doubt.
I have forgotten what I meant to have said ahead.
Not at all forgotten not what.
It is not whatever not is said
Which they can presume to like
If at no time they take any pains
Not to like it.
This is how I remember however.
Anybody not anybody can remember however but it does.
Not make any difference in any way.
This is what I wish to kindly write.
How very well I will at night
As well as in the day-light.
I could just as well remember what I saw
Or if not I could just as well remember
What I saw when I could.
The thing I wish to tell
Is that it makes no difference as well
As when there is this not this not to tell
To tell well or as well.
I have not thought why I should wish beside
Coming again as coming again.
They could write three to one
Or not two to one but which is not which
If they ask more than any fourteen.
Fourteen is however they like but not for me.
I am very capable of saying what I do.

I wish that they could not wish which nor do they.
I know what I say often so one tells me
Or if not I could not look again.
Might it be whichever it is
It is not my custom not only to think of a whole thing.
Does it make any difference which one they decide
Of course it does of course it does.
Alright let us think everything.
I have begun again to think everything.

Stanza VII

Now should or should not if they call with it
That I could not not only hear but see
Say when with spitting cavalry
She tears all where with what can be not now
They could be called to hurry call or hear or hair
Or there
Not only with nor welcome
Can they come and climb a vine
In place of chairs in place of chairs in place of chairs.
I could have thought I would think what with
What not not with only that
It is just as much noise as said
Or if not only which I cannot come again to combine
Not only fairly well but mounted.
I do not need the word amounted
Oh not at all
He knows when she came here
For which they can in all which all which called
Perhaps enchain perhaps not any name
For theirs will come as used
By this it is not only I mean
I mean I mean is always said again.
Remember what I said it is not just the same
Or not with only stretched.
In a little while he meant to perceive
For which they can or can not do
Do believe that I will say it used to be like that.

I wish to well assure it did not use to be like that
Not only that it did I did I did and did or do
Which can they come to for which they knew you
They knew who knew you
Every little while I often smile
And all which can come which they will approve
And not only not soften
But just as fairly often
Can they not come to say what they can do
I do very much regret to keep you awake
Because you should be asleep
But even so it is better to stay
And hear me say that is right here
What not only which they care
This can be made a reason why
They will be welcome to arrive and cry
They could do which they care.
Now to come back to how it is not all alike
Since after all they first
Since after all they were first
Best and most.
Now listen often cautiously
Best and most is seen to sweeten
Often often it is eaten
Much which much which much they do
Come and do and come for you
Did I not tell you I would tell
How well how well how very well
I love you
Now come to think about how it would do
To come to come and wish it
Wish it to be well to do and you
They will do well what will they well and tell
For which they will as they will tell well
What we do if we do what if we do
Now think how I have been happy to think again
That it is not only which they wish
It is as I have said a resemblance

To have forgotten as many times they came
That is to say we said
This which I said which I said this.
I said that it did not make any difference
And it did make this difference
As it made it made it do.
This which I mentioned made not only why but often
Now I have lost the thread of how they came to be alike.
Not only why if not but with their cause
Of course their cause of course because they do
I had been certain I would a little explain
Which can they do.
When I look down a vista I see not roses but a faun
That is to say the fields after hay
Are ploughed after hay
Not on the day
But just after the day
Like alike when it is chosen.
I wish never to say choose I choose
Oh not at all not while they like
Not while I like alike but do they
They may be often not declared as mine
For which I can not very well think well
Because just now I do not think well
Of at all.
She can be right to think that the sun
Not only does not fade but makes it less faded.
She can be right she often is always
This is what I said I would say
I say it as well as ever naturally
Because with which they would investigate
That they could not take a chance
Not to not to not to make no mistake
Not which at once to do.
It is often however they like
That they make it do.
I refuse ever to number ducks.
Because I know by weight how eight are eight.

Oh yes I do.
And a stanza too or a stanza two.
How do you do very well I thank you

Stanza VIII

I wish now to wish now that it is now
That I will tell very well
What I think not now but now
Oh yes oh yes now.
What do I think now
I think very well of what now
What is it now it is this now
How do you do how do you do
And now how do you do now.
This which I think now is this.

Stanza IX

A stanza nine is a stanza mine.
My stanza is three of nine.

Stanza X

I have tried earnestly to express
Just what I guess will not distress
Nor even oppress or yet caress
Beside which tried which well beside
They will not only will not be tried.
It is not trying not to know what they mean
By which they come to be welcome as they heard
I have been interrupted by myself by this.
This can be which is not an occasion
To compel this to feel that that is so
I do not dearly love to liven it as much
As when they meant to either change it or not
I do not change it either or not.
This is how they like to do what they like to do.
I have thought often of how however our change
That is to say the sun is warm to-day because
Yesterday it was also warm

And the day before it was not warm
The sun as it shone was not warm
And so moreover as when the sun shone it was not warm
So yesterday as well as to-day
The sun when it shone was warm
And so they do not include our a cloud
Not at all it had nothing to do with a cloud
It had not to do with the wind
It had not to do with the sun
Nor had it to do with the pleasure of the weather either.
It had to do with that this is what there had been.
It is very pleasant that it is this that it should have been
And now that it is not only that it is warmer
Now very well there is often that they will
Have what they look when they look there or there
To make a mistake and change to make a mistake and change
To have not changed a mistake and to make a mistake and
change.
Change the prophecy to the weather
Change the care to their whether they will
Nothing now to allow
It is very strange that very often
The beginning makes it truly be
That they will rather have it be
So that to return to be will they be
There will they be there with them.
I should often know that it makes a difference not to look
about
Because if to do they that is is it
Not which it makes any difference or.
But just what with containing
They need or made so surrounded
In spite of in a delay of delayed
It is often very changed to churn
Now no one churns butter any more.
That is why that is where they are here.
I wish I had not mentioned it either.

This whole stanza is to be about how it does not make any
difference.
I have meant this.
Might it be yes yes will it
Might it not be as much as once having it
Might it not only be allowed
And if not does not it bring back
Or bring back what is it
If they bring it back not for me
And if it brings it back for me
Or if it brings it back for me
So and so further than if.
It is easy to be often told and moved
Moved can be made of sun and sun of rain
Or if not not at all.
Just when they should be thought of so forth.
What they say and what they do
One is one and two is two
Or if not two who.

Stanza XI

I feel that this stanza has been well-known.

Stanza XII

Once when they do not come she does not come
Why does she not come.
She does not come because if she does not come
Not only this.
They can be thought and sought
But really truly if she need to
But which they make in which and further more.
It is not by the time that they could be alone.
What is the difference if he comes again to come here
Or to come here to go there to them
Or which they do which they do well
Or which they do not do well
Or more than which they do not do well

Stanza XIII

There can be pink with white or white with rose
Or there can be white with rose and pink with mauve
Or even there can be white with yellow and yellow with blue
Or even if even it is rose with white and blue
And so there is no yellow there but by accident.

Stanza XIV

Which would it be that they liked best
But to return to that it makes no difference.
Which would make no difference
Of course it makes a difference
But of course it makes a difference
And not only just now.
Whenever I return to this it is dull
And not by what I do
Or if by what I do
It is this that they like that I like.
I have wished to think about what to do
I do not have to wish to think about what I do
Nor do I wish to have to think about what they do not do
Because they are about out loud.
After all what is a garden.
A garden is a place in which
They must be in which
They are there and these.
This is not what to say to-day.
I have wished to be as this.
And I have and am as so I said I wished.
What could they use they could use
What could they either use
They could either use or use
If it is usual or is it usual
To be usually there.
It does not make any difference
That which they like they knew
Nor could it make any difference to use two.

After it was known to be is it as they knew
Think well of think of a difference
Or think well of think well of a difference.
They can be they can be there can be hours of light.
Light alright the little birds are audacious
They cannot kill large barn yard fowl.
How often have I seen them and they were right
How often have I seen them and they were not able to delight
In which they do.
It is not often necessary to look to see.
Not often necessary to look to see.
How easily she can can be there
Or how easily easily declare
Which they can be able to share
That they can can they bear this.
Or can they bear that.
I wish I could be rich in ways to say how do you do
And I am.
Or not only when they can venture to not remember
to prepare
Not only when they do
If not as not in which arrangement they concur
It is might it be easily mine.
I will not be often betrayed by delayed
Not often
Nor when they cherish which not often
They will come come will they come
Not only by their name
They could however much if however much
Not only which they come and cause because
Because of all the rest.
It is not only that they manage mine.
Will they be mine if not only when
Do they cover to color when
If they color when with then
Or color cover with whether clover
Can cover a color with clover then.
It is not safe to use clover as a name

When thinking of balsam and balsam is not only not the same
But not now the same.
In spite of which they tell well
That they were right.

Stanza XV

I have not come to mean
I mean I mean
Or if not I do not know
If not I know or know
This which if they did go
Not only now but as much so
As if when they did which
If not when they did which they know
Which if they go this as they go
They will go which if they did know
Not which if they which if they do go
As much as if they go
I do not think a change.
I do think they will change.
But will I change
If I change
I can change.
Yes certainly if I can change.
It is very foolish to go on
Oh yes you are.
How could one extricate oneself from where one is
One is to be one is to extricate whichever
They can be not for this any for an occasion
Of which they are remarkable as a remembrance.

Stanza XVI

Be spared or can they justly say
That if that if they will after all it will
Be just as if they say
Not only not they might but they will do
This they will do or if this will they do if
They will not only if they will not only will

But if they will they will do this.
For this thing to think it a thing to think well.
Having found that not only theirs or rather that
That it did make a difference that they knew
Now they know but none only which now they know
They know this.
They did if they had known not only know this.
But which can they be known this which they wish.
I had no doubt that it a difference makes
If there is doubt if money is about
I also know but which I know or worry
If when they give and take they give in a hurry
But which of which of this there cannot be a doubt
That if that could if it could come to be about
That if they did know this just as they had
Will as they had will to be worried still
Or not only not necessary a necessity
I wish to say correctly this
I wish to say that any day the roads a roads
Will they be roads they say when if
In not only not obliged to leave it well
But which if they can be to recollect
Oh yes not only which to gather to collect
They do try so to have the wind to blow
Not only not here but also not there.
This which I wish to say is this
There is no difference which they do
Nor if there is not or a difference which
Now which as which we should not add to now
No not indeed
I wish to say that they could eat as well
As if when now they heard when now
They had it had it when now
This is what which I did do say
That certainly to-day to hear to get to-day
That which as yet to-day is a relief to-day
Oh yes it is a relief to-day but not
Not without further ought or ought.

Now they need mine as theirs
But when they heard refuse a difference
Not any one has ours now.
Not in that way oh no not in that way
Come thought come thought of me.
I am always thinking that if in their way
If in their way it is if in their way
Insist if in their way
So could in of course shine but not wires shine
They can complete this time will will this time
There or they could in no doubt think.
This which I do I know or only only say say so.
This which has happened is my sand my sand my said
Of course my said why will they manage this wish.
Now I wish to tell quite easily well
Just what all there is of which to tell
Immediately increases hold as told
Or can they better be better be known
I have thought in thinking that is walking
That the way to be often more than told in walking
Is after all as much as told in walking
That they as well will be just not to have
Theirs be theirs now. It is not only this a change
But theirs might be
I have lost the thread of my discourse.
This is it it makes no difference if we find it
If we found it
Or which they will be brought if they worry or not
Without which if they begin or yet began
Can they be equalled or equal in amount
When there is a doubt but most of course
Of course there is no doubt.
I have said that if a cuckoo calls
When moneys in a purse in my own pocket
It means wealth
Moreover if the cuckoo to make sure
Comes near then there can be no doubt if doubt there be
But not by this to see but worry left for me

Makes no doubt more.
Does it can be it does but I doubt it.
After this I think it makes no difference what their
characters are
What you have oh yes I thank you
What I have is made to be me for mine
I should not please to share oh no of course.
But not to go into that is not in question
Not when no bird flutters
Even if they yet can be yet here
This which I think is of this kind around
They will be called to tall
No one is tall who has not all
They have not only all
Which is which they can
They say August is not April
But how say so if in the middle they can not know.
Think how well to like everything.
I wish to say that I made no mistake in saying any day.

Stanza XVII

I feel that often in a way they link
Not if they should and shouted
But can they mind if which they call they went
Or not only not of course
But not only welcome more.
There is no doubt that often no alone
There has been a waste who quiets a waste
But which they will they wish
I say yes readily steadily do either do
But which they will in theirs to theirs deny
Not to have been ruffled by success
Or either or they can not be inclined
To gather more than give giving is foolish
Spending is a pleasure gathering is making
Bettering is no delight they like to light
Of course they like to light it.
They like not to explain but add a day.

Very likely to take away if to take away
Before it was of importance not to go now
But not now.
I wish to think to refuse wishes
Also not to refuse trees or please
Not to refuse bells or wells
Not to refuse does or could
Not refuse made to be with which to go
Made to be minding others leave it so
What I have said is this I am satisfied
I have pride I am satisfied
I have been worried I will be worried again
And if again is again is it
Not to be interested in how they think
Oh yes not to be interested in how they think
Oh oh yes not to be interested in how they think.

Stanza XVIII

I could make at it most or most at it.

Stanza XIX

I felt that I could not have been surprised
Or very much as they do
If it is that I remember what
What do they if they never dot
But which is not warranted by what
What will they have as is if not to mean
It is not difficult to either stand
Which on account if without flavor
Shall they be shamed with generation
They can leave it half as well.
I wish to remind everybody nobody hears me
That it makes no difference how they do
What they do
Either by our or either by at all
This is why no doubt it followed better
To have no one eight or eat before.
This which I think is this.

I think I could do not without at night
Not only not a moon
Can they be told as well
This what is what I do can come
Not to prevent which when they mean they come
Or not only for it.
All this is of no interest
If indeed there is no right
No right to keep it well away
Just when they do or either not delight
Can they collect or recollect their way
Not only which but whether they can plan
I wish to say I do not not remember every day
Not I
Not even when I try or why
Not even well not even very well
Not even not without which not even more
Should or just yet recollect
That they that is not there
Even not there much as it is much allowed
For them to come for them to come.

Stanza XX

I wish to say that who could
Or just as well as welcome
This which I know now I know followed how
How did it follow of course it followed how did it follow
Not only no tide is perplexed
But they will perplex less in usefulness
Useful or noon can well be kept to right
Should they not care for
What will they care for
I like to think how every one thought less
Of what is this when even is it know
Mine is what is it mine is
Shall they not often be not only made a way
Make and made made stayed.
This which I have remembered is made known

Shall they should always know
Or less the same
They can be often thought made quite well.
She could in which instance for instance
Leave love alone.
They could call dears early years
Or not only their care but with their care
Can she be well to manage more or less
However much it is however much alike
This which I know is what I know
What I know is not what I say so
Because I wish to draw drawers and drawing
Or can they even call and talk well and welcome.
Think how often it does not change and mind
They are not glad to sit and find
Find it nearly out.
It is not nearly nearly so
It is not fairly nearly nearly so.
For which it is not often not only better that they like
In which is reason.
In reading a long book which I look
In reading and reading a long gay book
I look
This is what I see with my eyes.
I see that I could have been made the same
By which by in which name the same
They can include in tries and tires
And feel or felt can it not it inspire or inspires
They could in no doubt know.
I cannot well remember whether it was yesterday that I wrote
Or if yes of course naturally I should
Wait another day.
Or have waited another day.

Stanza XXI

I wish always to go on with when
When they meant then

Stanza XXII

Not only by their hope I feel so
Can they be not with all a wish to know
That they will well declare to do so
But which they will as much as all delight
For this in their way one way one way to know
That it is never gladly to be so
In which it is in often which it is
As they will not be made with them
To be here with them
A stanza can be bought and taught
If not why if not will they or can he will they not
It is not often that they narrowly rejoin
Or as the way or as their way
They will be finally as their way
Can they be finally as their way.
This which I know I know that I can do
Or not if not if I can do if not
If not at all they were not only not to wait awhile
Or which if which is better than only not better
It is possible that only if they did and could know
They would happen to arrange that they could not be
Which they had thought and taught
Or meant to teach or meant
Happily it is sent.
This makes no hope of better than it should
They were pleased that they were well well meant
Or left to have no other as it were
Left finally for it.
I wish to announce stanzas at once.
What is a stanza
When I say that often as a day
I feel that it is best to know the way
That if upon the road where if I went
I meant to feel that is if as if sent
She if I came and went

Or well what is it if it makes it do
Not only which if not only all or not alike
But it is it is just like Italy
And if it is just like Italy
Then it is as if I am just like it
That is make it be.
There is no necessity to make it be if it is
Or there is not any real making it do too
Because if which it is or just to know
To know and feel and may be tell
Is all very well if no one stealing past
Is stealing me for me.
Oh why oh why can they count most
If most and best is all
Of course it is all or all at all
Most and best met from there to here
And this is what I change.
Of course I change a change
Better than not.
This that I must not think I do
Which is to do but met and well
Well when I like when they like.
There is no hope or use in all.
Once again to try which of a choice.
Theirs is no sacreder in sacrament
For finally in disposes
When they plan
This which I can do.
I wish once more to begin that it is done
That they will fasten done to done
Or more nearly care to have to care
That they shall will and can be thought
To need most when
When whenever they need to mean
I mean I mean.
This which I do or say is this.
It is pleasant that a summer in a summer

Is as in a summer and so
It is what after all in feeling felt
Can they not gain.
Once again I went once or more often than once
And felt how much it came to come
That if at once of one or two or one.
If not only if not one or one
One of one one of one which is what
What it is to win and find it won
This is not what I thought and said
I thought that the summer made it what it is
Which if I said I said I said it
And they were using used to as a chance
Not only to be which if none it was
It was used for which for which they used for it.
I wish I could say exactly that it is the same
I will try again to say it if not then
Then not alike there is no then alike
There is no then not like alike and not alike
But that.
This which I mean to do again.

Stanza XXIII

Often as I walk I think

Stanza XXIV

But this does not mean that I think again.

Stanza XXV

Which can be which if there
This which I find I like
Not if which if I like.
This which if I like.
I have felt this which I like.
It is more then.
I wish to say that I take pleasure in it

Stanza XXVI

A stanza can make wait be not only where they went
But which they made in theirs as once awhile
Can they be close to wishing or as once
Can they not be for which they will
As wish can be more reconciled for them
In which respect they will or so
Or better so or can they not be meant
All which they plan as theirs in theirs and joined
Or not be left to rather wish
But which they will in no way
Or not in any or rather in any way
Theirs which they leave as much
Or better not or better not all alone
Not if they call in early or to care
Or manage or arrange or value
Or relieve or better like
Or not at all as nearly once compared
Or made it to be gained
Or finally as lost
Or by them not detained
Or valued as equally
Or just as much established by their lost
Or finally as well prepared
Or can they not without them which they cherish
Not only by them but by the time
Not only will they but it is one to like
Or manage just as well as if
As if they planned theirs which they know
Or in as well as do
Would they be more contained
To leave it not for them
By the time that all of it is better
Once more to have it do it now
As moon-light
Naturally if they do not look or go
They will be always there or not at all

Not why they went to manage as it is
Felt which they like or as a place to go
They could feel well they went
They could not partly show
Just which or why it is
Not only as it is more than they thought.
They will arrange to claim
It is not only which they will or know
Or changing for it partly as they if.
If it is only made to be no delight
Not only as they finish which as well as they began
Or either not to on account
Not only why they will
Or often not often not often not
It is of more than will they come and can
Can they be here if after joining
They will partly in at once declare
Now in no haste if not now in no haste
As just when well supported they need it
Not only if they use but do they use
And might they not be well not be well inclined
To have not which they manage or amuse
Not which they fragrantly and always now
If when they know mint can they not know
Not often will they better have than either or
Not only when they share
But even when they share
There is no mending when they delight
When they delight to have or can they share
It is partly this which is not only mine
Or not not only mine
Or will they not
Or will it be meant to attend
Or follow rather than not follow now
Just and in that way or rather not to say
They will not happen to be often disturbed
Or rather not to have or love it so
They should not can or will not do their way

Of better not to like or indeed can it matter
Not even not at all
And so marking it as once and only once
In which in which ease
Can they be mine in mine.

Stanza XXVII

It is not easy to turn away from delight in moon-light.
Nor indeed to deny that some heat comes
But only now they know that in each way
Not whether better or either to like
Or plan whichever whether they will plan to share
Theirs which indeed which can they care
Or rather whether well and whether.
Can it not be after all their share.
This which is why they will be better than before
Makes it most readily more than readily mine.
I wish not only when they went

Stanza XXVIII

To come back to a preparation
Or fairly well know when
It is as much as if I thought or taught.
Taught could be teaching
Made in which is strange if strange
That they will otherwise know
That if indeed in vanishes
Theirs where they do not even do
What after all can be which can they call
They can call me.

Stanza XXIX

A stanza should be thought
And if which can they do
Very well for very well
And very well for you.

Stanza XXX

This is when there are wishes

Stanza XXXI

Of course he does of course he likes what he did
But would he mind if he liked what he did
Would he like it better if it did not matter
Not only if he liked what he did
But often just as well
If he did not share in seeing it there
And so might they not only be so
But which if once more they were readily
But which they like.
In there as only as a chance
They could control not only which they liked.
I think very well of changing
I do think very well of changing this for that.
I not only would not choose
But I would even couple it
With whatever I had chosen.
Not only can they gain
But might they gain
They should as they manage
They should share as they manage
They should be often as they manage
Or can or mean disturb
Or as they like
Or leaving it fairly well
Much as they wish or will
Fairly nearly or alike.
I could if I wished have spoken
Or rather not not only
I could arrange and amount
Or for which they would keep
They could have all or could they have all
But in the adding of a place

They will commence intend amuse
I would rather not come again.
It was often so much better than I thought
I could not manage with anguish
I felt that there was partly as a share
To prepare
Liking and liking it.
It is of no importance
Not a chance than which they will
For which they know in no renown
Ordered and colored there
They will not only reach it but pleasantly reach it.
Which is why they will add it as they call.
They could be left to mean
Or rather might they rather be left to mean
Not only why they like but often when
All of it has been shortened by being told
At least once at a time
For them they will know variously
That is not only meant as meaning
But most of all as most of all
Are there not only adding theirs as when
When could they call to shorten
Shorten whatever they are likely as very likely
To have not where they planned
But just as much as place
A place is made to mean mischief
Or to join plan with added reasoning
They could without without which
Might it be without which
All of it which they place to call
Not only made differently indifferently.
I could do what I liked
I could also do whatever I liked
I could also as much
I could be there and where
Where can that be
Where can that be

As not only when but always
Always is not however why they like
There are often opportunities to be chosen
More as they like if they at once they like
Not only as not only used to use
Should they in every little while remain
Not only as much as if they cause
They never need cause distress
This which I have I add to liking
There is no necessity to decide an amount
Of whether as they do they might do this
Because whenever and if why they like
All which or which is strange
Need not in the meantime mean any end of when
Not only for the wish but as the wish
I manage whatever I do I manage
I could not only like hers but mine
Mine can be or if whether they could do this
Might they not only be in season as a reason
Should they have found it or rather not found it again.
This which is what can be what they need not only for them
They will be plainly a chance
Plainly a chance
Could they not only like it
Can they not only like it
Or if they can not only like it
However can they even be with or without it
For which as better or a just alike
As planned.
Once when they could be choose as a choice
They will feel that which as moreover
It is an opportunity
Not only in exile.
What is exile or oh yes what is exile.
Exile is this they could come again
They will be felt as well in reason
As which if which they planned
I could be ought I be without

Without doubt.
Now a little measure of me
I am as well addressed as always told
Not in their cause but which can be they need
After which can it be
That this which I have gathered
Can gather must will change to most
Most and best.

Stanza XXXII

Could so much hope be satisfied at last
Can they be lost as lost
Can they be carried where as found
Or can they not be easily met as met
By which they use or very much they like
Made while they please
Or as much.
When very often all which can they call
Or further happen can they not call
Can they not be without which help
Or much or much alone
It can be not only why they wished they had
Finally funnily or as funnily at one time
It is more than they relieve caution
But which they might.
Might they be thought very often to have come.
Neither in mean nor meaning
They will be presently be spared
They will all feel all which they please
They will not either share as they manage
No plan which can they like
Often which more than for which
Can they like
I feel very carefully that they can be there
Or in no pretence that they change the time
Time which they change.
It troubles me often which can or can it not be
Not only which in and because their share.

Let me listen do when they mount
Or if not as they did.
Did or call.
Rest or restless or added rest
Or which or which might they
Made to be arranged for which
Might they be pleased if after often
They could not share tried
Or even places.
They can not acknowledge or add it.
Fortunately to rest.
They can be well enough known
Or by the time they wished
I can not often add add to welcome
Please be not only welcome to our home
Can they call a terrace terrace
And also pleasure in a place or garden
Or does which can does it please
Can they please if they must
But which which is that it
So very often is not only left and right
But can they add to which whichever
Can they not only please.
It might be called all hills or nationality
Or not be even always
Being placed as can they wish
It could be often helped
Help or it is as more
This is the story.
A head should be a chimney
That is well or welcome
It might be made in forty years or two
One for a man and one or one a woman
And either having neither there.
Each one is not at all in their replacing
Alas a birthday can be squandered
And she will always please
Or call it well alone

Can they never try to otherwise attain obtain
Or feel it as they must or best.
Best and lest they change for all.
I regret that it is one to two
Or rather yet as change maintain.
Or please or rather certain a mountain.
Not nearly dangerously.
It can be often thought to be helpful
She can not change what she can not change it for.
It is why wondering do they or lilies fail.
Growing each day more pale that is the leaves do.
Otherwise there is a pleasure in adding
A doubling of their plan.
They will add adding to their tender care
And often as if much as if
More of which as if
They would be well pleased well pleased as if
They could in their hope be carefully.
I wish now to state it clearly.

Stanza XXXIII

They can please pears and easily
They can easily please all easily
For which they please

Stanza XXXIV

There is no custom to know yes and no
They could be easily meant to be fairly well meant
To have in which and can they try
But which and which they carefully rely
Upon it.
In no mean happening will they call
They will never differing from will refuse
And remain meant to please
And so remain meant to please and delight
All of which they meet
All meant in adding mine to mine.
In which case most and best is readily read

Nor do they mean to find and please
As they mean which they add to adding
Or better still add which to add and apples
And to add bless and caress
Not only ought but bought and taught
In kindness.
Therefore I see the way

Stanza XXXV

Not which they gather.
Very fairly it is often
Which they have as is their way
They will rather gather either
Either or which they can
For instance.
It is a curious thing.
That now.
As I feel that I like
That it is as much as
It is exactly like
When I found it easily easily to try
And it is as if it were
As very much alike
As when I found it very much
I did then not wonder but wander
And now it is not a surprise as eyes
Nor indeed not if I wonder
Could it be exactly alike.
This I wish to know.
If you look at it if you look at it like it
It is very simple it is just as alike
By this it is more not only this.
Little by little it comes again.
For which no one need more need like it
It is like it not only here but there
They could which ever they
What I wish to do to say
It is as much as if like it.

This I can like as not dislike.
It has often been said in landscape historically
That they can tell.
What if they wish they can tell.
As I am wandering around without does it matter
Or whether they oblige that they see other
They can if they manage or at best
Either a color
I think well of landscape as a proof of another
I wish well of having brought to think
Which is why well at first.
At first I did not know why well
Why quite well as much as well
Why it could be just as well
That it is like or if and like
This landscape this color.
What is a landscape
A landscape is what when they that is I
See and look.
Or wonder if or wander if not which
They come slowly not to look.
I think so well
Of when I do
Which I consider
Which they do I do
Or if not if at all
When I see over there
There where they color do not call or color
Not if water not if not if water
Not if they could be a part
Think well of gather well
I come to wish which if I add or wish
It is now that however it is now
This which I think which it is the same
When unknown to fame I needed which I did not claim
For them or further made for them
In which they added claim to blame
I wish to say that not only will I try

I will try to tell very well
How I felt then and how I feel now.

Stanza XXXVI

What is strange is this.
As I come up and down easily
I have been looking down and looking up easily
And I look down easily
And I look up and down not easily
Because
It is this which I know
It is alike that is.
I have seen it or before.

Stanza XXXVII

That feels fortunately alike.

Stanza XXXVIII

Which I wish to say is this
There is no beginning to an end
But there is a beginning and an end
To beginning.
Why yes of course.
Any one can learn that north of course
Is not only north but north as north
Why were they worried.
What I wish to say is this.
Yes of course

Stanza XXXIX

What I wish to say is this of course
It is the same of course
Not yet of course
But which they will not only yet
Of course.
This brings me back to this of course.
It is the same of course it is the same
Now even not the name

But which is it when they gathered which
A broad black butterfly is white with this.
Which is which which of course
Did which of course
Why I wish to say in reason is this.
When they begin I did begin and win
Win which of course.
It is easy to say easily.
That this is the same in which I do not do not like the name
Which wind of course.
This which I say is this
Which it is.
It is a difference in which I send alike
In which instance which.
I wish to say this.
That here now it is like
Exactly like this.
I know how exactly like this is.
I cannot think how they can say this
This is better than I know if I do
That I if I say this.
Now there is an interference in this.
I interfere in I interfere in which this.
They do not count alike.
One two three.

Stanza XL

I wish simply to say that I remember now.

Stanza XLI

I am trying to say something but I have not said it.
Why.
Because I add my my I.
I will be called my dear here.
Which will not be why I try
This which I say is this.
I know I have been remiss
Not with a kiss

But gather bliss
For which this
Is why this
Is nearly this
I add this.
Do not be often obliged to try.
To come back to wondering why they began
Of course they began.

Stanza XLII

I see no difference between how alike.
They make reasons share.
Of which they care to prepare
Reasons which
I will begin again yesterday.

Stanza XLIII

If they are not all through

Stanza XLIV

Why have they thought I sold what I bought.
Why have they either wished that they will when they wish
Why have they made it of use
Why have they called me to come where they met
Why indeed will they change if no one feels as I do.
Why can they carry please and change a choice
Why will they often think they quiver too
Why will they be when they are very much further
Why will they fortunately why will they be
It is of no consequence that they conclude this
For which it is in no degree a violation
Of whether they will wish
All can see why they see
Will they see me
I do I think I will will I be will I be
Fortunately for it is well well to be welcome
It is having left it now
They mean three to change.

I will include I will allow.
They could having see making it do
She can arrange our a cloud
But they think well of even
I wish to remember that there was a time
When they saw shapes in clouds
Also as much.
And now why why will they if they will
See shapes in clouds but do not
Do not draw the attention of any other one to it.
They can be even used to it.
What I wish to remember is not often whether theirs
They can be living what there is
Or rather why they are inclined
To leave hills without clouds
To be covered with haze
And to be transparent not in mist
But finely finally well
They could be such as there
Will they or will they not share
They might be thought to be well caught.
I feel that I have given this away.
I wish now to think of possession.
When ownership is due who says you and you.
This as they feel this.
They will accomplish willows with a kiss
Because willows border rivers.
Little rivers are in a marsh
Having forgotten marshes and trees
Very much or very well who sees.

Stanza XLV

I could join if I change.
If I could see which left it that
Can they call where they will as left.
But which they like.
Oh yes they do oh yes which they do like
They need any stanzas any stanzas there.

They could be seen as much.
Leave it as much.
Can they be fairly fancied.
Can they be as much as fairly fancied.
No one knowing how knows how.
I feel.
I feel that they will call it tell well.
If not in joined can they release.
Or yes not as to please.
I wish once more to think of when a wagon
Can they not yet be drawn.
Of which of whether if they need.
Of whether yet they share.
Can they be seen to care.
Colored as oxen.
It is not only here that they know oxen.
Oh yes oh no it is not only so.
It is that they will leave and leave.
And might they can they leave.
If they can leave to have to come to leave
They will come which can they come
I will not think some come.

Stanza XLVI

Why are ours filled with what it is
That they reach mine.
They do and if they do will they be theirs as mine.
And if it is night they could just they share
Might they be one I won
Or can they be which if they could.
I must say all which is as if they had met.
Often adding had makes leaves as well
If gathered when they fell they usefully are used
It is not why they like they readily grow.
She chose one to two.
Heliotropes are through through the air.
And yet I saw her choose
Find it for him

I saw her choose.
She could be thought to be.
They like alike.
I wish to notice that they are at all.
To arrange to choose.
As much as for which use.
I will mention it.
She has been very well known to like it.
I can say that it is a pleasure to see the bouquet.

Stanza XLVII

I will can I request.
That they should offer this.
I have not felt to which can be true
That they will yield if either if they wish
Will they to you

Stanza XLVIII

I have been astonished that black on white
This I have been astonished that it thickens
But why should black on white
Why should it thicken.

Stanza XLIX

I wish moreover that I think again.
Will you follow me as much as thought
How could when any know.
What could I do if when I felt I left.
Left it to her to do.
Not much which I can know
In which I know.
I can be often or rather awfully doubtful
If I can be seen to have been wished
Wished well as while.
For all which all that while
Can it be not alone not liked.
They can be no occasion to leave roses
On bushes.

But if not only why I sit
But can be not only if only why I sit
I can be often as much as ever
More can they like.
I think that if I feel we know
We cannot doubt that it is so
They cannot with which they change
Once more they see that it is I
Brown is as green as brown is green for me.
This makes me think hardly of how I learn.

Stanza L

Can you please please me.
Can he be not only why I like.
Which they shall never refuse to hear
I refuse to hear her.

Stanza LI

Now this a long stanza
Even though even so it has not well begun
Because whichever way they can contrive
To think well will it be
Need I remember what I carry
Can I plan this as strangely
Can I can I not even marry
May I come further than with which I came
Can I completely feel can I complain
Can I be for them here.
Can I change sides
Can I not rather wish
Can I not rather wish.

Stanza LII

There has been a beginning of begun.
They can be caused.
They can be caused to share.
Or they can be caused to share.
Should no one have thought well or well

For which no one can change frighten.
Or plainly play as much.
Or nearly why they need to share
Or can they just be mine
He has come to say I come again.
They could really leaving really leaving mine.
I could not only wish
I could not only wish for that.
I could not only wish for that here.
It is very rarely that there is a difference known
Between wood and a bone.
I have only felt that I could never exchange
They will be thought to welcome me.
I am coming.
They will not be annoyed that I am coming
They will be glad
They will have often had it.
I have often admired her courage
In having ordered three
But she was right.
Of course she was right.
About this there can be no manner of doubt.
It gave me pleasure and fear
But we are here
And so far further
It has just come to me now to mention this
And I do it.
It is to be remarked that the sun sets
When the sun sets
And that the moon rises
When the moon rises.
And so forth.
But which they meddle or they will as much
They have asked me to predict the weather
To tell them will it rain
And often I have been a comfort to them.
They are not a simple people
They the two of them.

And now they go just as well
As if they were used to it.
Which they are.
They go into the fields.
There can be things to do
Which there are
Which there are in the fields
And so they have not sought to change the noon or the moon.
But will they ask a question
Most certainly they are not divided.
It is often thought that they know
That it is as well to know years apart.
Ask quietly how they like it.

Stanza LIII

By which I know
Can they like me
Not only which they know
But they will wish
They will wish which they know
And now and ours not at all
Can they be once with which they will declare
And place and ours know
They can with better which they even well declare
That they can change or is it in a union.
They can be finally to find that they
Can see and since as one can come.
Come one as one can add to come
Come which they have
Once more to add feeling to feeling.

Stanza LIV

Could she not have it as they made an impulse
He will not feel that it is made to change
They will conclude that parts are partly mine.
They will have will.
Will they come when they will

Or will they wait until.
If when if not when will they.

Stanza LV

I have been thought to not respect myself
To have been sold as wishes
To wonder why and if and will they mind
To have it as it is and clearly
To not replace which if they as they do
Can they content can they be as content
For which they will if even be it mine
Mine will be or will not be mine
Rather than mine and mine.
I wish to say
That it is her day
That it might be well
To think well of it
It is not often led or left
But whichever and whenever
Can they not only be
All mine.
I often think will I be thought to know
Oh yes of course I will be known to know
I will be here I will be here and here
It may not be that it is I am here.
I will not add it more and not
Not change which is a chance to leave it.
I can be often very much my own
I wonder why
Is it that is it here.
Can I but not to try
I can cradle not infancy but really
What I can.
They can collect me.
They can recollect me
They can if mine is mine.
Not even mine is mine.
Mine which is mine.

Nobody knows a name for shame.
Shame shame fie for shame
Everybody knows her name.

Stanza LVI

I could be thoroughly known to come again.
Often if I do
I come again.
As often if I do.
I could not change often for often.
Which I do.
Often for often which I do.

Stanza LVII

I have often been doubtful if yes or no
Annoys him.
Or is it only the setting sun
Or the chairs softening
Or the direction changing
In which they see why I do.
Might it not be only what they like.
I like what I like.
Can they not like what they like.
But very often he means nothing.

Stanza LVIII

By which they might.
I have often thought that it is right
That they come if they might
But which they change from their right
To imagine which they might
If they tried.
Not only why they wish but if they wish for us
It can be not only that only that is gone
But which they might not only
But which they might if not only
Once when they went to go
But which if they might

I think might they if they might.
I wish would wish that they might
If they might they would not if they wish.
Would they if they not only would they
But which if they would if they might.
Now then how strangely does it happen
If better not not only now and then.
This which I wish to say is this.
It has happened which I wish
Now and then.
This which I wish is to happen
Now and then.
This which is if I wish.
Which is to happen now and then.
The way to change this to that
That is now this now this to that
Or that to is it this to that
Or no not indeed that.
Because of this or is it this to that.
By which I mean to say dozens to-day
Yesterday or dozens also
Or more over more alike and unlike.
This which I wish to say once which I wish to say
I wish to say it makes no difference if I say
That this is this not this which I wish to say.
But not not any more as clear clearly
Which I wish to say is this.
She has left roses and the rose trees.
By which I mean to say is this.
If it had happened not only were they not remembered
But if at all not even if at all
Not even if at all if if they were not remembered.
I could have not only which if which if whenever.
I can choose what I choose that is to say not chosen.
Not only if they were not having been where.
No one can partly go if I say so
However much they could
Did if they would.

But which they much as if they were
To add more he comes here
As if he came here from there.
I wish to say I could not remember better
Nor at once
By which I mean
Could they come here I mean.
They have come here.
Each one has come here once or twice as that.
Make it three times and they will remember better.
Not only that but will I will I be
Partly with it partly for it
Partly for three
Not three but three times.
And not three times three but any three times.
This can be wrong it can have happened well
Very well it can have happened.
That if they came four times
They had come three.
It can not even not be better yet
Not as yet
Should they be thought to be.
By which no one means what I do.
I do not partly do not.
Or if not partly do if not
I come back just to think is three not more than four.
Or is three not enough if four are not more.
This can they try.
This that they can come here
Of course this that they can come here
Of course no more no more of course no more.
Can we know that there is this difference.
No more not any feel it known as well
This which I tell this which I tell.
Do you delight in ever after knowing.
But which they mind that always as they come
Not only heard it once but twice but not again.
They could they could if not their ground

They could if they could not stand their ground
They will be shelves of shelves
Rather be only rather with their shells of shells
Or best or needed needed in their praise
Of course we speak very well of them
They have been able too.
Able to be able not only ours abound
But which could which tell if no one.
No one adds palpably to their amount.
There there they read amount account
Cover better a wasp came sitting gently
To tell of a coincidence in parting
And to be well kept in which after which
In doubt in no doubt now
But they feel grapes of course they do or show
Show that grapes ripen ripen if they do
Not always do if not if not that they often do
But which if which
There is no advantage.
I wish to say again I like their name
If I had not liked their name
Or rather if I had not liked their name.
It is of no importance that I liked their name.
There can be this difference.
It can be one number that is written
To mean that it is another number which is to follow
Or it can be that the number which is to follow
Is the number that is written.
The only thing that helps one with that
Is memory.
And sometimes I remember and sometimes I do not
And if I remember can I be right.
Or is it best to look back to be sure.
After all they could not know which I said.
And they are not forgotten but dismissed.
Why should one forget and dismiss which one of this.
This which they add that I do.
I could never believe that I could not happily deceive.

Stanza LIX

Some one thinks well of mine.
Some how some think well of mine.
Well as well but not as well as mine.

Stanza LX

Next to next to and does.
Does it join.
Does it mean does it join.
Does it mean does it mean does it join.
If after all they know
That I say so.

Stanza LXI

I wish once more to mention
That I like what I see.

Stanza LXII

By which I might if by which I might.
There can be only which if once I might.
If once I might delight.
If if not once if not I might delight.
Either is other other is order
Or if they ordered that no one is to wish
Not only wish but which
Not only not not only
Not if they not if they wish.
They not only had they been
But they had been as much as disappeared
They could candles water-falls if they liked
They could call bread easily bread
They could even do as they wish
They might even do that
Not only as they like but when they find
Not easily when they find
Not more not easily when they find
They carry which they carry

They add not only not that which they add
But they must not add will they
If they need no one to force them
To declare
That they will not add if they change.
They should not easily delight.
Not only theirs.
Should they increase if they could like it.
And can they call for them.
I wish moreover to say
That I was not surprised.
I could remember how many times there was an interval
In not only which way but in any way
They can nearly not be known
Not more than once at all.
After which can they lead.
I need no one to rest well
They will call a light delight.
They like sun-light day-light and night as a light
They also like day-light
They also need their light.
They also will show it as their light to-night.
They also will remain if they remain and leave it.
As they might.
This which I say has meant this.
I cannot call it that there is no doubt.
Is there if I say what I do say
And say this.
Moreover if they stretch as not only will they do it.
But can they not only not do it
But not have done it.
Not at all.
She can be appointed.
It can be an appointment
They will not nearly know
Which they can care to share.
I wish I wish a loan can they
Can they not know not alone

Not know why they can
As it is of no use
That they sat as they say
In a way as they did not sit
In a way to stay.
This which has been as this.
They have been with them there.
Can they not care to spare
That they were if they were there.
This which I remember
I do not remind them to say.
Of all of them one of them.
Which can birds lay.
They like to be as tall as more anymore.

Stanza LXIII

I wish that I had spoken only of it all.

Stanza LXIV

So far he has been right
Who did alight
And say that money would be plenty.

Stanza LXV

They did not know
That it would be so
That there would be a moon
And the moon would be so
Eclipsed

Stanza LXVI

Once in a while as they did not go again
They felt that it would be plain
A plain would be a plain
And in between
There would be that would be plain
That there would be as plain
It would be as it would be plain

Plain it is and it is a plain
And addition to as plain
Plainly not only not a plain
But well a plain.
A plain is a mountain not made round
And so a plain is a plain as found
Which they can which they might
Which they tell which they fill
Could they make might it be right
Or could they would they will
If they might as if they will
Not only with a will but will it
Indeed it will who can be caught
As sought
For which they will in once
Will they they will
Might they not will they will
Much which they had they will
It is of ever ready pleasure
To add treasure to a treasure
And they make mine be mine
If once when once
Once when they went once
In time
They can be used to prove
They can be well they have been
Shove
Shove is a proof of love
This which they have been
And now they add this which
In which and well they wish
They add a little pink
To three which were as well
For which they do not add
A wish to sell
They will add will they well
Well if they wish to sell
Well well if they wish to sell
Who adds well well to a wish to sell

Who adds well to a wish
Who adds a wish to well
We do.
We had been as well
And we do.

Stanza LXVII

I come to gather that they mean
I do.
I come not only well away
From hound
A hound is a dog and he has known his name
Another dog and not a dog
Not a dog in his name
I wish not wish not will
Will they be well as well
And for it no one need a moon
A moon at noon
What was it that she said
A sun and moon and all that loss
Divide division from a horse.
She said I would she said I did
Not only which not only why.
Why will be well as well reject
Not to neglect
Not if they wish alike to try
Can they as well be well
Will they as by and by.
Which I can say
Which I can to-day
To say
Could they come as they go
More than which whether it is best
Do do so.

Stanza LXVIII

I need not hope to sing a wish
Nor need I help to help to sing
Nor need I welcome welcome with a wind

That will not help them to be long.
Might they not be there waiting
To wish this
Welcome as waiting and not waiting more
I do not often ask I do not wish
Do not you wish
Do not you either wish
Or ask for all or more.
There is no hesitation to replace
Which when they will and can they will
By and by he asks it not to be there.

Stanza LXIX

Be made to ask my name.
If I think well of him be made to ask my name.

Stanza LXX

I cannot leave what they will ask of it
Of course of course surely of course
I could if I could know
Does if does it seem so
Can we if I am certain to be sure
That it is as I do
It should be changed to place
They can if will they care
They can if as it could
Be not more added.
I cannot if I ask be doubtful
Certainly not
Nor could I welcome change as neither change
Nor added well enough to have it known
That I am I
And that no one beside
Has my pride
And for an excellent reason
Because I am not only
All alone
But also

The best of all
Now that I have written it twice
It is not as alike as once.

Stanza LXXI

There was once upon a time a place where they went from
time to time.
I think better of this than of that.
They met just as they should.
This is my could I be excited.
And well he wished that she wished.
All of which I know is this.
Once often as I say yes all of it a day.
This is not a day to be away.
Oh dear no.
I have found it why will he.
This which I wish to say is this.
Something that satisfies refuses.
I refuse to be ought or caught.
I like it to be caught or ought.
Or not if I like it to be ought or caught.
This is whatever is that they could be not there.
This is an introduction to Picabia.
When I first knew him I said
Which was it that I did not say I said.
I said what I said which was not in him.
Now who wishes that said is said.
Not him or women.
Or sigh or said.
I did not say I wished it was in him.
Not at all I said forget men and women.
Oh yes I said forget men and women.
Oh yes I said I said to forget men and women.
And I was not melancholy when I thought of everything.
Nor why I thought.
Of course nor why I thought.
That is enough not to have given.
And now if why might I.

The thing I wish to say is this.
It might have been.
There are two things that are different.
One and one.
And two and two.
Three and three are not in winning.
Three and three if not in winning.
I see this.
I would have liked to be the only one.
One is one.
If I am would I have liked to be the only one.
Yes just this.
If I am one I would have liked to be the only one
Which I am.
But we know that I know.
That if this has come
To be one
Of this too
This one
Not only now but how
This I know now.

Stanza LXXII

I think I said I could not leave it here.
I can be all which when whenever either or
Can they be which they like for.
Or will they worry if they lose their dogs.

Stanza LXXIII

Can she be mine oh can she can she be
If they could welcome wish or welcome
But they will be surprised if they call me
Yes can they gather or they gather me.

Stanza LXXIV

It is not what they did which they ask me
Or for which if they could they give to me
Not ducks of Barbary

Because if ducks there be
They will be eating ate or would be
Better known than if not.
Will they leave me.
Of course if rather gather.
Can they be inestimably together.
It is as very long to be indefinable
As not for which not if for which
They wish.
Thank them for gathering all of it together.

Stanza LXXV

I like that I like.
Oh yes not if not I like
Can they be a credit a credit to him
I like
If when if I like
Not if in choosing chosen.
Better which pronounced which
If which plus which
Can they be I like.
I need no one to prefer refer
Or rather mainly used.
More which they change.
Let us be thoughtful
Let us know that if they could be known
They would be gathered if at known
Say so
Manage not only not to say so.
Saying no
I wish to think that I had thought.
I had not only loved but thought
I had not only even called and taught
I had meant will or well of fishes
I had thought could they call me well of wishes
Can they be only once allowed
But which they frame.
Having not had a picture

Which to frame
Now I do know a name
Why when they like a man called Susan
He will regret allowed for Susan
Or just why why if they can not try.
It is to gather other than he knows
When once is often
Who will begin again.
Ours are ours all ours are hours
We had a pleasant visit with not mine
Would they have been would they have been in time.
Should they if they.
They will gather love is mine.
Butter is mine.
Walls are not only mine
Will they or if they had rather
Been when they were to find mine.
They will not either leave it all to chance
Or yet no one knows movements which having fallen
He fell to seat it where they could be all
No one imagines all for either all
Red or not red
I do dislike to hear
That red is here.
Thank you kindly for the thought
That either we are bought.
Or really not to be bought
By either caught or ought.
Should shell fish be well baked.
Or either will they all in origin.
Remain remained tall.

Stanza LXXVI

I could not be in doubt
About.
The beauty of San Remy.
That is to say
The hills small hills

Beside or rather really all behind.
Where the Roman arches stay
One of the Roman arches
Is not an arch
But a monument
To which they mean
Yes I mean I mean.
Not only when but before.
I can often remember to be surprised
By what I see and saw.
It is not only wonderfully
But like before.

Stanza LXXVII

Now I wish to say I am uncertain if I will if I were every day
of any day.

Stanza LXXVIII

It is by no means strange to arrange
That I will not know
Not if I go or stay because that is of no importance
No what I wish to say is this.
Fifty percent of the roses should be cut
The rest should bloom upon their branch
By this means no one will mean what they pleased
And even if they are occupied they are content
To believe mind and wind, wind as to winding
Not as to rain and wind.
Because because there is very little wind here
Enough of rain sometimes too much
But even so it is a pleasure that whether
Will they remain or will they go even so.
I wish to know if they only mean to know
By me by you they will as readily maintain
That not by me by me as well remain
I wish to know if it is well to be by now to know
That they will remain if they might mean I know
If once if once if I might mean I know

That not which only if which only now to know
Know not in mean known if it is not only now
They could in gather mean if they meant mean
I mean.
This which I wish to add I wish to wish to add.
Can I can I be added which is not any wish.
To add.
I which I wish to add why should add not rhyme with
sad and glad
And not to talk to-day of wondering why away
Comes more than called to add obey to stay
I wish I had not thought that a white dog and a black dog
Can each be irritably found to find
That they will call us if if when if added once to call
Can they be kind.
We are kind.
Can they be kind.
I wish no one were one and one and one.
Need they think it is best.
Best and most sweetly sweetness is not only sweet.
But could if any could be all be all which sweet it is
In not withstanding sweet but which in sweet
Can which be added sweet.
I can I wish I do love none but you

Stanza LXXIX

It is all that they do know
Or hours are crowded if not hours then days.
Thank you.

Stanza LXXX

Can she be not often without which they could want.
All which can be which.
I wish once more to say that I know the difference
between two.

Stanza LXXXI

The whole of this last end is to say which of two.

Stanza LXXXII

Thank you for hurrying through.

Stanza LXXXIII

Why am I if I am uncertain reasons may inclose.
Remain remain propose repose chose.
I call carelessly that the door is open
Which if they can refuse to open
No one can rush to close.
Let them be mine therefor.
Everybody knows that I chose.
Therefor if therefor before I close.
I will therefor offer therefor I offer this.
Which if I refuse to miss can be miss is mine.
I will be well welcome when I come.
Because I am coming.
Certainly I come having come.

These stanzas are done.

WINNING HIS WAY

A NARRATIVE POEM OF POETRY (1931)

Or her way.

It is very often to have it warmer to content her.

And they went their way.

They were chosen to be won their way.

This is the way that it was done.

One.

But why will they be away when they are at an advantage. To stay, and be welcome.

Finding it lonesome.

They are willing. To be welcome.

Finding it handsome.

They are willing to be able.

To be welcome.

A fortnight ago. Or so. They went away. Carefully. In intention.

A man sitting upon a tree and they were singing to me. In welcome.

He was perfectly aware that he was sitting there. And welcome.

He knew that. Roses. Are. Red. And. Roses. Are. White. And Roses. Are Rose. Colored.

This was Lolo. And his dog. And his mother. And his house. And his house. Which is. Not let. To Frederic.

All call. Frederic. He names no names.

Frederic rolls.

James follows.

Lolo waits.

Herman states.

That he is very well to-day.

And so they are happy.

To share.

Their care.

Of Lolo.

It is very wonderful to be three in a queen.

And soften. Three in a same as in a day.

And so thankfully.

The friendship between Lolo and every one was very strong.
And they were careful to do no wrong.
When they visit him.
For they do. Very truly.
All who have been here have been here patently.
It is all about that they are thoughtful.
And strange.
And comfortable.
And pleasurable.
In the meantime verbs do not mean stares.
He stares.
A friendship in order to have time must be ready to. Be known.
Or else. As well.
Why did they think. For them. Or may be. They will. Have them.
Unequal. To them. In a light.
Many share a cradle. Or think with them. In mine. For which. They like. As much. As they must.
It is in this way. That they feel. That they know. That they are celebrated so. Exactly. For in referring. To up and down. And walking. They should. Be a belief. Of their account. Or much. Which is in vain.
They will call louder. Or their mother. With it. Will it. Be in vain. Rather. They must not dislike having it. Because it is a re-lief. To choose plants. As flowers.
And this changes from friendship to day-light.
It is miraculously see. That they should. Plant seeds. For shrubs. As will as well. As strewn. Or can it be occasionally.
In which valid. As in thank.
As in seen. They in shrank.
Pour in wean. Or in share.
Is in more. Than in a share
Of renewed thanks. For this thing.
That they have. As they wish.
For anything.
Be careful of borrowing. Or without them. They know. The

color. Of a carnation. Or in indeed. They can be nearly. Thinking it in grapes and pears. All understood. As yet. Not. Found.

And so friendship ceases.

Suppose they could be found.

To answer. She predicted.

Now first he had no enemies, and no one thought but he could. Surely it is advantageous.

Secondly no success. But satisfaction. Rightly. In exactly. She would. Be. Legal. She. Would. Be. Bare faced. As. Occupying. Or. May be. They do.

Thirdly. All or out. Pages. Pages. May be strewn. With fortune. Or best. With acknowledgement. In better yet. Than four. And most. And so. He trusts them.

Third. She knew better than that Fred and Frederic and Freddy would not ask.

Do be dear to them.

And now can poetry. Be acknowledged. Supreme.

How are ours said.

For them. And bread.

And leaves. And most.

Should arouse. Choice.

Of treasures.

She can be balanced fortunately.

As different differently.

As soon.

All closed. In their recollection.

In Reference. To. And noon.

Noon. Can be chosen.

Friendships. May be left. To them.

These are the facts.

She did see.

That places may make.

A widow of her.

She had. Been.

A widow. As well. As. A mother.

And a daughter. A wife.

A wife can be thin. With a dinner.

She can come readily. With. Them.
In whether. Or indeed. After.
Or rather.
A cold. And gather.
If she meant. Migrate. In living.
Rather. Where. She had been.
In living. Further.
It was a little. Then. That. Her father.
Had not made. It. For him.
Her husband. Had. Been. Having rather.
More. Than had been. For her father.
She made. Nobody. Thin.
They could. Come. In.
Like that. In their hand. With. Him.
She made it rather. Be thin.
That they came farther. Her father.
Had been. There. With. Him.
She was married to their father.
They were married. By their mother.
Not by him. Not with him.
Not for them. Not by them. With. Them.
She was married. To their father. By him.
He had been a father to them. Because he had been married to
their mother. Before them.
And so this was their father. Married to their mother. The fa-
ther of their mother. Was the father. Of their mother.
They were both married later.
And this made them. Leave him.
She was left. By them.
She was left. Because he had been.
Dead as the husband of the mother and the daughter of the
father. They left them. She was left. With them.
He had been. Her father.
She had been left. By him.
He had been. Her husband. With him.
And now it was. Not necessary. To think.
This of. Them. Who had been. Left with him.
And so she was the mother. Of them.

And the widow. Of him.
And the daughter. Of them.
And the rest. Of them.
Because. She was left. By them.
And she had been. With him.
She had been left. With them.
She had been left. A widow. By him.
Because he had been dead. By then.
And she had been. Left. With them.
She had had a father. Her father had a mother. Her brother
had been dead. By him. And the mother had been a widow. With
them.
And so they had been left. With them.
She had a father. He had a daughter. With them. She had been
a widow. With them.
They had left her. For a mother.
They had left her. With the other.
By them.
With the mother. By them.
They had been with the mother.
Of them.
It is all likely. In their hope.
Any way. In which. To love. That may.
Be have. And leave.
A cow. Alone. And a sheep.
Which can have quail.
Made not its name.
She was sent. By them.
To sit. Along.
She said. It was. The habit. To.
When. They could.
Friendship made no noise for them.
In elegance.
Made in prepare. That the truth was told.
Did Florence know.
These are the facts.
And they were. Not interested. In the facts.
He says. She says. They were not thinking. Of these facts.

And so. They move. To love. And live.

With them.

The mother. Has a hen. Which is better fed. Than then. When. They had. Other things. To do.

And so. Seasons. Are not through.

She says. It is better. When. They are not. Together. Which is true. In summer. Rather. Than. In winter.

And this makes it alike. Smilingly.

It is an advantage. To have houses. Surrounded. By themselves. In their talk. Of their life. She may be. Not be seen. As they do not care.

For their fulfilling their share. Pleasantly.

It is an advantage. To have sold. Oxen.

Who is to share. What they have.

She is. To share. What she has. With herself.

In summer. And in winter. And they may be.

Next to nothing. She is. Very well-to-do.

But she is not through. With softening.

She is received. In coming.

And they will clash. By themselves.

Not to do. This.

They think. They thank. Well.

And ours. Seem. Mine.

Day birds. Sing quicker. But. Not. Longer.

It is by seize us. That they christen. Baby. With by. Caesar. Seize us. That they Christen. A baby.

Which. They do not have. Or. Come. Completely. Finding it. An aunt.

No one. Mentions. Ants.

How many can remember. Who left.

They make it do their. In trim. We were not photographed. With them.

A second praise. They have.

She likes. To do more.

With an. Aid. To be. With them. More.

All exercise. In interrupted.

But do they. If they leave.

But do they. If they. Leave.

They will. Think. That they more. Are moved.
By all. They bought. They fought. They caught.
With them. In bless. And care. With them.
In change. Because they can. Allow.
Them. To have. For them. Two cows.
No chickens. Even. Because it makes.
Too much. To. Do.
With it. It touches. Me.
To see them. See them be.
With them. For will they.
Love them. As they go. Away.
At once. As they know.
That an hour. Is so.
Well known. As. With. By them.
It is very pleasant.
To need all. That they give.
Them.
Just when. Will they like it. For them.

Paragraph 2

It may be. That she.
Felt that this. Was.
Had she been.
In. Engendering.
It was. That they. Meant.
Originally. Lament. In. And wish.
It is. Of not use. To ask. Why. They were.
Depending. On their. And. Now.
It comes. Slowly.
If they. Hear it. Heard. It.
Hours. Of intercourse.
Think sweetly. Of friendship.
It is attached to blame.
Should it. Classify. Undoubtedly.
A Narrative Poem. Of any bird. Singing.
She may doubt. If they do.
But they. Do.
She may doubt. If a narrative poem.

Of a bird singing. Which they do.
Or of sighing. Which they do.
Of singing. A narrative poem.
She may be. Fairly. Better. Too.
Which may they do. In cutting. It.
In two.
A nest of names. In orange.
In oranges. Fruits have been called.
Fruits. As they. Readily.
Make it their. Politeness.
In ours. In peals. Of their hope.
She will sit. And complain.
There can be come altered. As at.
A marriage. Of pleasure. And predilection.
In. Will they pause.
All kindly leave their home.
Birds. Never. Are frightened. By singing.
With them. And. Is. Along.
Will they scatter with. Saving.
With them. Well along.
With them. In saving. Them. Along.
So that. They scatter. For a ladder.
A ladder. Owe. Own.
It is. In. With a. Song.
Better. Rather.
Come seriously. For. Rather.
A little poem. Says. A Turk.
Can. Work.
Also. A place.
To play.
In changing.
Theirs. In place. Of theirs.
As changed. From. Rather.
In. Or. A place. To work.
What happened. In the rain.
It was seen. To rain.
And so. A country. The country.
Prospered.

After they had managed to see very much of them.
One in once. In erring.
A sweet grass. Is eaten. In hurrying.
And also. Spoiled. But. Not destroyed.
By the habit. Of. Which. He had.
Having made a mistake.
A mistaking rain. For a plate.
Or else. Rather a noise.
As understood. Urging.
By that time.
It is. In the meanwhile. Easy.
To admire the house.
Having returned to not having seen.
Him. He was present. In the garrison.
As a sergeant. And no one. Was mistaken.
This was not. At a time. Of war.
But in peace.
When there was a meeting they said they knew nothing.
Of any one of the ones. They had. Known everything. And
so. No. Distress.
Coming to a couple. In feeling.
Could they be. Most happy.
In winter. Yes. But. Not there.
That is what she said.
And they. Could cloud.
Rain could. Please. Allowed.
Paper.
How could a narrative poem.
Be broken up.
How can feeling. A brook.
May be shaded. And whether.
It is more. For the. To see.
That it is intermittent. To. Close.
But it is. Without vexation.
To be seen. More. Than. They told.
Their best. Is now. With. Butter.
Made. In vain. For their. Excitement.
Radiate. Interest. In leaving leaves.

About. Which may be useful.
There is no doubt. That if.
It is known. That she went.
In no way. Can. They resolve.
That it is. Public.
Now imagine. So many. People.
Seen once. May be. Sure.
How can. Any one. Differ.
In being. Reserved. That. Now.
They are. Public.
Now they are. Public.
Which. They may be.
Doubtless. They are.
Now could it be thought.
It would be. By them.
Holes in the ground. Made by. Gophers.
Are not. Credited. By them.
With having. Hurt strawberries.
And roses.
Now what is the difference.
Between those. Everybody. Knows.
And those. Others.
How do you do. Very well I thank you.
A continuation of the. Narrative Poem.
Winning. His. Way.
A poem of poetry.
And this. And friendships.
The problem resolves itself. Into this.
Does a poem. Continue. Because of. A Kiss.
Or because. Of future greatness.
Or because. There is no cause. Why.
They should wish. To know. Why they.
Were prepared. To be so. As they were.
Very likely.
This is the. Problem. They are. In the.
Public eye. And they. Were not surprised.
And yet. Not yet. Who chose. Who goes.
They can feel. And kneel. To take out.

Morning glories. From strawberries.
Even in that way. Tiring themselves.
Very well. It does good.
It is simply stated. The way is.
That they say. Should it be led.
Away. To be careful. To be. Understood.
To ask warily. Of awaiting.
At no time. Is there time.
Between. And having. To be.
Between. And waiting. To be.
In seen. Often. Relating.
Before. To say. Before.
And clothe. Them. With glory.
Very well. I thank you.
Should they choose. That they knew.
Everybody repeats partly. That they knew.
That the glory. Would be all through.
The days. Of their having. This glory.
It is. In no way. An accident.
So they say. And they know. Who knew.
Nobody knew. They did. Not know.
That they were partly so. In their.
Glory.
This is the way. They start. Not wondering.
But referring. To this. That is.
What is. Partly through. Their glory.
But which. Beset. By names.
Comes for them. In remain.
To move. They more. Before. They think.
That he is busy. With this.
And that makes. A pleasant noise.
Of paper. It is their pleasant allowance.
Of its approach. How is it possible.
That everybody knows. Just how. To say it.
When. The time comes.
And so. They satisfy it. With more.
At once. And glory. Thank you.
So much. For this.

I like to like. To have. This.
Which I do have. This.
And therefore. I understand.
That I meant. This.
By this. I mean. That it came.
To being. Mine. And so.
Do you think. It is. That.
That they have. Why certainly.
One would not have thought. It.
It is by this time. That they mentioned.
For them. One another.
In order. To soften. Something.
And to begin. There is no known.
To begin. Their. Adding. Intending.
In time. To be. Sown. It is.
Rather remarkable. That he had planted.
Them in squares.
At the corner. Of squares.
Thank you. For answering.
When to win. Is a way. To weighing.
He was able to be easily.
Contented. And grateful.
For not having been. Deceived.
By this. Or by that. Thing.
And thanking. For something.
And so. Now. A poem.
Is in. Full swing.
A narrative poem. Is commencing.
A poem. Entitled.
Winning his way.
A poem. Of poetry.
And friendships.
When the time comes.
It makes them clearer.
Or as much. As either.
It could be a cover. With paper.
Which makes. Them. Prepare further.
Undeniably. Ours. Are much better.

Or for that occasionally. In really.
Their account. Of it. Made easily.
For them. To give them. Pleasure.
Or more alike. To be sure. Which is.
Not without them. As needed.
They may be for. And to take.
Almost readily. Just this. Allowed.
Or by. And gracious. Gone with.
And by. That amount. Or may be.
All of which. They counted.
Out loud.
Should they be called. By me.
Back. By me. Or. Not.
But with. A glance. For this.
In excellence. They should shout.
With bait. For excellence.
No one. Needs. Imitate. Suggestion.
Of. They remind.
That paper. Will imitate. The feet.
Of a dog.
When it does. Make it. As if.
It were. To cover. Tapestry.
Here. And. There.
How many roses are allowed.
By them. To mean. That it is.
Politely. Accepted. To mean.
That they will. Come to believe.
That it is seen. That they will.
Be accepted. As. Determining.
Can you repeat. We glory.
In. Our success.
And. They will. Date. The name.
Of. Winning. His way.
As yesterday. For to-day.
To-morrow. Gradually. To stay.
Or. Authority.
Not a narrative poem too readily.
A poem. Of poetry. And. Friendship.

Of poetry. Winning his way.
A narrative poem. Of poetry.
What is the announcement.
Please. Authorise. That they never knew.
That it was true.
When the time comes. They will place.
The piano. There.
She may be. Really. Very fairly.
A pleasure.
In receipt. Of their. Announcement.
That. He had grown. Woods. And flowers.
And may it be. Partly. Better.
To be there.
Surely. It is. Not a mistake.
To be famous.
Nor without. It. For them.
At once.
Should they. Borrow. More. Butter.
Nor rather. Ask. For mushrooms.
Nor even dally.
By a harness. For them. Or stairs.
She may. By all accounts. Be after all.
Fairly careful.
In lightly. Or lightly.
Asking. It to be. As they may.
It is very well. To have it. Well selected.
Nor ought it. To be. A bother.
To them.
For carelessly. To be. Watched.
Nor had they.
Lost seed.
It is. Winning a way.
Which makes. Poetry say.
A narrative poem. Of poetry.
And friendship.
Sustained. By their impression.
In often told. This. In amount.
Was it their pleasure. Of course.

Poetry of his all.
This is known. Best of. All.
She is winning her way.
And for this because by reason of this.
Her son is here in this way.
She was not necessary but for this.
For this. She was necessary.
Not for this. For her son.
But because of this. She was necessary.
And so. They will. Do so.
A paper is disturbing.
Than this. With this. Than this.
She was is necessary. For this.
And in winning. Her way. She was.
Not winning. A way. Because of. The way.
In which. She was necessary.
She is winning her way. If it is useful.
To have her stay. In winning her way.
Winning her way. Winning his way.
A long narrative poem.
Of poetry. And friendships.
Winning his way.
All. Of his day. Winning his way.
Naturally. Winning his way.
She is winning her way. By this way.
And as she is sleeping. The paper. Is moving.
Winning his way. A poem.
A long narrative poem.
Of poetry. And winning. His way.
The poetry. Of paper moving.
Because. She was sleeping.
Winning his way. A narrative poem.
Of poetry. And friendships.
And not. To be removed. As leaving.
Winning his way. A narrative poem.
Of poetry and of friendship.
Winning his way. In. Coming.
Why have they not made.

A pansy perfume.
Since pansies smell. So delicious.
They are beautiful. And. Delicious.
Pansy perfume would be delicious.
A narrative poem entitled.
Winning his way. A poem. Of poetry.
And friendship.
A narrative. Should be. A poem.
Telling. Of poetry. And friendship.
And it should have the name.
Of. Winning his way.
This is such a narrative poem.
It is a narrative poem.
Of poetry. And of friendship.
And it is to be known as. A
Narrative Poem called. Winning his way.
In the place. Where. They might.
Be abandoned. A father might be.
Abandoned. A mother. Might be.
Abandoned. A sister. Might not be.
Abandoned. Nor a brother. Nor a daughter.
Nor a son. Nor a daughter-in-law.
Nor a son-in-law. Nor a grandmother.
Nor a grandfather. A place where.
A mother. Might have been. Another. Mother.
And a father. Might have been. A father.
Indeed. They are. Established. In this.
Country. A very long time. As well. As ever.
This country. Is here. And is. Very well known.
And established. As having been here.
And not. As well established. As having been.
As well known. It is very well known. Now.
It is well. Hoped. That roses smell.
And they. Mean. To bloom. In so.
Great a quantity. That. There. Will be.
More. Than. She is able. To cut.
And place. In the hope. Of this.
It is very happily. Very well.

That there is to tell. This.
And also. If it is. A kindness.
To call. To her. And tell her.
As often. As much. As when.
As will. As they. Pronouncing. Then.
In question. For them. In direction.
Will you kindly. Do so.
Nor need. It be. As well. Not. As she.
Interrupts. Fame. Or. Famously.
Ninety-nine. Allowed.
It is very well known.
That they follow.
Very well known. Remains.
Leave it. As comfortably. Very.
Much better. Than whether. It is.
Made or had been made. As ever.
Very well known. As ever. Better.
The thing is this. They go. And they. Gather.
Clover. For themselves. And their. Animals.
They have to have. As aid. To work. For them.
They will also. Dismiss. Her.
With them. And Mathilda.
How many places. Are birds. Forsaken.
None. Here.
A narrative. Does not. Necessitate. Mingling.
Fame. Pressure. Determination. Resolve.
And accord. Also. Neglect. And. Retirement.
Wherein. Do they differ. From them.
Three. Times. In asking.
He said. They did. She did not.
He did not. They did. Not.
Differ. From them. Relatively.
Because. For their. Or. For their. Sake.
It is better. To have. As a measure.
Their. Pleasure. Yes. Their pleasure.
Their. Pleasure. Is their measure.
Which makes them. Divining. Or more.
At once.

Finally heated. By them. For. Walking.
She may. Happen. To be having. It. As often.
And they will. Leave them. To call. For them.
To soften. Their. Having heard them. Call them.
As often.
It is. By fame. That. They know. Them.
They will awaken. Them. By feeling.
That it is. Their feeling. That makes them.
Feel this. In them. For them.
And so. A Herald. Comes. To come. Then.
For them. With Withstanding.
It is called. By them. Of them. For them.
With. Often. How many are hurried.
What is fame. And how do they feel.
They feel. Very well. And. Very often.
And. So forth. With reason. Because.
It would be. Not allowed. To be.
Different.
And so. They imagine. Finely.
Winning his way. Is a narrative poem.
Of poetry. And description. Of friendship.
And fame. And soften. And theirs. As well.
As often.
Winning his way. A narrative poem.
I can be deceived. In the direction of a sound.
And so can he. When startled.
Winning his way. A narrative poem.
Of poetry. And of coming. To come.
Pleasantly.
This is done. Daily.
And. More. Often.
Winning his way. A narrative poem.
Of poetry. And of. Friendship.
It is not mine. Than they wait.
For instance. May they incline.
To be wondering. Why there. Is a difference.
If there is.
It is fame for them.

For them. They may. Be. agitatable.
This is the way that they miss or dismiss.
One or twenty or twenty-five more. Of them.
On account. Of melons. Water buckets. And. Or roses.
What makes to-day. The day. For marrying.
The same. As yesterday. For their cutting.
The hay. Be or. As well. As if. They could. Be seen. To need.
It. To-day.
This is the meaning. Of varying. Or.
Winning his way. A long narrative poem.
This is Wednesday. The day. When the bakery. Does not
open all day.
He was known. As they. Stood.
Why are they different. In this. From them.
Hardly and true. That. She. Is kind.
For them. Did. She know. Yes. A. Little
But not. Enough. No one. Does. Who.
Can. Belie. Arrive. Belie arrive.
They will. Thought. Shares. Arrears.
And so. They might. Have been. Instrumental.
In being. Famous. Because. They were.
Reasons. There were. And. In stays.
Of reasons. For. Their use.
Let us think well. Of bliss.
Winning his way. A narrative poem. To say. Of poetry. In.
This way.
Should. Choice. Reason. A name.
Choice Henry. And. Victor. And Linden.
Arthur. And Imogene. And Vermillion.
A silk. Is made. For three.
In just. A minute. To be. Theirs. Only.
What is it. That they know. That they. Can know. Of him.
Yes. Beware. Yes. Or where. They. Leave it. To its care.
For fortune.
This is all. Of a will. They. Believe in. Their pretty. Home.
In which. They are. Famous.
It was a mistake. To ask. Them. To stay.
And think. Of it.

Because. It is used. As a pleasure.
Because. It is. Used. By them. As a. Pleasure.
Relieve them. So that. They will. Not hurry.
Because. If they. Marry. He will be able.
To be here. By then.
Could they think. Very often. Of.
Doing this. For them.
At least. In meaning.
They will. Add this. To their. Pleasure.
Because. It is. By no means. All. Theirs.
All. Who ask. To go away. Come.
Come. Readily. This is. Asking. For them.
Oh. Two. And sighing. Because. Of dreaming.
And also. A little seizing. In mowing.
It is better. To be moved. So that. They come.
Winning his way. This is. A pleasure. For some.
Nobody thinks they said. It there. As often.
It may be taught. That they will. Do this thing.
As often.
Or more. Than they allowed.
He will be a soldier. Partly. Because. He has to.
Partly. Because. Until. He will.
He will. Ask to. Go. As. He is going.
This has nothing. To do. With winning.
His way. Winning his way is a narrative poem.
It was made to make a noise.
By the action of the wind.
And this. Might have been. A disturbance.
By either asking. Or giving butter.
Which. They sell. As milk.
But which. They carry further.
And ask nothing. Of either.
Which. They sell. As milk.
For which. If they give. More.
Than they ought. Acacia is. In bloom.
And smells sweetly. In honey. And milk.
And so. They may. Have everything.
To-day. Or determining. That. They may.

It is intentional. That they gather. Whether.
There is delight. In. Whether. There is.
Delight. In either. Or rather.
Please them. By anything. With adding.
It is a hope. Of kindness.
A narrative poem. Should narrate wishes.
He wishes. That it were possible. To have grown.
As many roses. As there have grown there.
By his efforts.
He wishes. That it. Had been. Done.
As he wishes.
He wishes. That. They will be careful.
Of whether. There is more. Than which.
They will add rather. More. Than there.
Can be. In awaiting. That. It will come.
For them. They will. Be. Often. Readily.
Careful. Of whether. There is. Restraint.
Could there. Be changes. In whether.
They will use. What. They have. Bought. To them.
As very likely. That. They will.
Because. It is. Exactly. What. They had. Desired.
In this way. They will. Not be used. To. The name.
Their. Name. Is known.
That. Their name is known. Makes fame.
Any one. Can remember. Anything. With pleasure.
And so. They often. Add. That. They are. Famous.
Winning his way. A narrative poem. Of poetry.
And fame. And friendship. And worship.
Out. In the house. In which. They make.
Mention. Of whom. All. Always. Expels.
A great many. Can sell. Forty. Pears.
Or even. Always. Everywhere. In pleasure.
Prevailing. If the reach. With them.
As they make. Politeness. Jerking.
It is. Manifestly. To their relief. That it rains.
Because. Besides. Closing. The shutters.
Which were open. They will. In diction.
Say. Purchase. Is persuading.

And they will allow. Cows. To be quiet.
And indeed. Hens. Accidentally. Chosen.
Which were. Without intention. Given.
Not. In their behalf. Oh no.
A daughter has. Been led. To be wed.
And though. Although. There. May be. Grief.
No one tries. To arouse. Them. As.
By use. Of their. Wedding.
Never. Again. Will she mention. Marrying.
Because. It is of course. All which.
When they cough. They think feather and whether.
As extortion.
Oh will they be quickly ready. To go. There.
Where they think. They are. Grateful.
What is fame. They think well. Of their.
Being met. With little Lilly. At. A neighbor.
And she asked. Was she. Looking. Better.
All of them. Are agreeable. In that setting.
And so. They will be. Profitable. Not more.
Than. On their account.
All day. They announce. Wednesday is after.
Tuesday. Because on Wednesday. The bakers. Close.
It is very often. Their pleasure. To think. Of winning.
Winning his way. Is what. There is. To say.
Of a narrative. Poem. To be written. In this. Way.
What it. Should be. Is on. This side.
And they add. To it. A list. Beside.
And he asked. When he was given. How.
Many. Are there. In six. From seven.
And they meant. Not to quarrel. At all.
Because. They are always. Happily smiling.
In having. Them. Which. When one. Came.
Made it be that they asked. Are you. Coming.
Winning his way. A narrative poem.
Of poetry and fame. And admiration.
And so. They need. Knees. For. Thinking.
How are. Hours. Made. For. Forty. Winning.
Leave. Well enough. Alone. And ask them.

To marry. Geometry and their addition.
Think well. Of changing every name.
Winning. Won. Wanted. And begun.
His. Harping. Holding. And. After. It.
Way. Without. With them. With all. Of them.
Variety. A narrative poem. Is pointedly.
Their.
Possession.
Who can manage to apply this.
And I never noticed. What it said.
On the other side.
On this side. It said. What it. Should be.
And a narrative poem. Of poetry and friendship.
Is commenced.
Winning his way. A narrative poem.
Telling of the difference. That makes. Fame.
A long narrative poem. Of how. They did. Feel. About it.
Made a way. Winning his way. A long narrative poem.
Of poetry. And fame. And differing. About it.
Should they just. Be the same.
A narrative poem. About fame.
Should they just have the same. Fame.
A long narrative poem. About poetry. And about. Fame.
What. In what. Way. Do they differ.
And. In what. Way. Are they. The same.
Those of them that have. Fame. From those of them.
That do not. Have. Fame. In what way.
Are they. The same. Those. Of them. That do not. Have
fame.
What is. Fame. That they. Have.
And what. Is different. In them. That gives to them. This.
Fame.
From those of them. That do not have.
Given to them. Fame. Or is it. Not the same.
Not. To have fame. As to. Have fame.
And are they. Who have fame. The same.
As those. Who do not have. Fame.
This is why. It is. The same.

A narrative poem. Of poetry. And fame.
Any change. Can be. That. Name.
A long narrative. Poem. Of poetry. And. Of fame.
Winning his way. A narrative poem.
Of poetry. And friendship. And fame.
And. A consideration. As to whether.
It is. Or. It is not. The same.
As not. Having. Had it. Nor. Enough. Of it.
Our having seen. And. It is not. Made. Indeed. For them.
What. Is she doing.
In going. Over there. And. Standing.
She will. Seat herself. Again. And go. On. Tapestrying.
And. This. Is no explanation.
Their. Pleasure. Their cause. Their. Ball.
Nor which. If it is. A standard.
It is. A hope. That. They can be.
Elected. As. At. Their. Present.
It is not. Of any use. To tell. It. At. All.
That he has. Dropped. His ball.
And. Has gone. Back. To a chair.
And that. Has bumped. The desk.
And. It has. Not made any. Difference.
All kinds. Of bought. And. Brought.
Nor. Indeed. Is it. A bless. The. Black chicken.
She has. Gone. As a task. And all.
Very. Well. I thank you.
This. Has. Nothing. To do.
With. Winning his way. In a cause.
Of it. Being. A first day. Of. An evening.
She can be. Scarcely. Conscious. Of. I guess.
That it is an. Offering.
But. It is. What. They may call. Pleasing.
Which accents. Theirs. At once. As. Pleasing.
Please. Find it.
The thing. That makes. Winning. His way.
Their. Pleasure. Is this. They. Can decide.
To abide. By its falling. And. If. It falls.
And. He waits. Then. He returns. And there.

Is. A hesitation.

Hesitation. Is a name. Of a waltz.

And so a narrative. Poem. Is. Interrupted.

By movement. By sound. By breathing. By leaning.

It is a pleasure. That very nearly.

Red. At night. Sailor's. Delight.

Red. In the morning. Sailors. Warning.

Rose is a color. That is lighter. Than red.

And rose. Can be. Almost. As light. As white.

She has picked. Very many roses.

A long narrative poem. Can. Refuse. Interruption.

And. No change. And. Placing. Theirs. As in. Referring.

A. Pleasure. Is in knowing. That the country.

Is beautiful. Even. If it. Is. Perfectly. Remembered.

Remember. How. They like it.

A narrative. Poem. In. Discretion.

They will smile. As at a circumstance.

Winning. His way. A long narrative. Poem.

Of. Poetry. And fame. And. Friendship.

Will. They come. To welcome. Them.

And will they. Find. Resemblances. Between. Them.

What is. It. It is. In their. Place. That they.

Come in. And leave. It. As it happens.

That. They will not control. Their. Hope.

Their. Help. Their. Appointment. Their enhance.

In kindness. Their help. Their use. Their part.

They will. Place. Mine. For. It. As. Well.

In. Spreading. More than choice. A frame.

Can. Make a noise. Easily. With aid. Of silk.

And slipping. Which they chance. To chance.

Smiling. A chance. To leave. It.

She is very busy. With. It. Which has been. Noisy.

A long. Narrative poem. Narrative poem. Which has been.
Dull.

In. Unison. More then. In. Indwelling. In. Winning his way.

A long narrative poem. Of poetry. And fame. And friendships.

Will they. Be mine. If the silk. Is slipping. And.

The frame is creaking. As they. Mean. To be. Pushing.
Nearer it. To her. Or farther. It. To her.
Thank you.
This is. The beginning. Of a. Long narrative poem.
A long narrative poem. Winning his way.
Not very far from Bilignin they said.
They have come. They are here. They will stay.
Thank you. They may.
Not very much. As well. It is unlikely.
That it is. Not unlikely. Because. It is.
What. They had. Not placed. Wherein.
When. All. The time. As much.
Which is. As much. Really.
Now think of two. Things. Fame. And. Roses.
Not think. Of anything. Fame. And. A dog.
In. Inside. With. An. Especial. Thought.
Of. Winning his way. A narrative poem.
Of poetry. And fame. And. Winning.
His way. That is. It is. That. Way.
There. He is. Doing. It. Again.
What. Is there. That makes. It. Be. Who is.
There. She has. Met. No women. With a black chicken.
What is. The difference. Between. A hen.
And a chicken. A rooster. And. A chicken.
In importance. With known. With. With known.
A narrative poem. Could tell. Something.
It tells. Of their feeling. That this. Is occurring.
What made. It be. Very likely. That even.
They knew. That they were. Going. To a. Wedding.
In their. Attempt. At. Watering. Pansies. In the evening.
It is needful. To expect. To sigh.
A narrative poem. Of poetry. And fame.
And watering. Vegetables. And Balsamine.
In the evening. With pleasure. And later.
With some suspicion. Of their. Honesty.
Some suspicion. Of their honesty.
A place. In it. For everything. Which.
They are placing. In a. Narrative. Poem.

Their kindness. And their aptitude. In learning.
For instance. Would they be interrupted.
Not. Very easily.
And so. There is. A narrative poem.
Of poetry. And of fame. Which is known.
As the poem. Winning. His way.
It was the occasion for their thanking.
They will be welcome having received making.
It be manageable by them for them.
What is fame. This is fame.
Who are famous. We are famous.
With this. As an. Effort.
May they. Be able. To find. It.
By. Being. Almost. With it. In. It.
Very closely. To it. And succeed. In. Having it.
That which. Has been put away. In the place.
Where. It has been able. To be. Found. And. Taken.
Leave fame. To those who are famous.
They will. Be found. To be. Famous.
Because. It is possible. For them. To add.
This. To that. In which. They come. To like.
May. They. Be as well. Able. To and add.
Them. To their. Relief.
For which. They thank.
This is a narrative. Poem. Of poetry. And fame.
There is. Fame. And there. Is. Poetry. And fame.
Poetry. By being. Brought. Too. To. Knew.
They will. Be settled. That. It is. Extraordinary.
That. Roses grew.
This is. A simple. Fact. And they may be.
Very much. As. They have. Made. Their. Liking.
There are two. Choices. They have taken. Them. All.
Nor will. They gather. As. They have. Them.
By. Which. They mean. They will. Have. More of them.
Some call it. By having. It. To be. Exactly.
As well. As if. They had. As much. More.
Of them.
Fame. Is expected. And. Unexpected.

Roses. Are unexpected. And they are expected.
Once given. The place. To have them.
So then. There is. This difference. In a garden.
Fame. Is expected. When it is. Not. In a. Garden.
It is expected. To have roses. If. There is. A garden.
It is unexpected. To have fame. When there is.
Fame. As expected. Which is. That. There is.
No expectation. In anything. Which. They do.
Thank you. If this. Is true.
Gradually. Fame is increasing.
Thank you. For thinking. Of this. This evening.
It should. Go on. In more. Than. They will.
Because. If it. Has. A place. Until.
They mean. That. They know. The difference.
He will. May be. They need. To place. A tree.
Before. A seed. That means. That they.
Will remove. The tree. Without waiting.
Insomuch. As they. Ask it. In their. Wedding.
As an interruption. But not. To fame.
They will. Think. Of everything.
In no need. To neglect. Looking. For. Something.
Which he has. And which. Not only. Has not been mislaid.
But not even lost. And in this way.
There is. No interruption.
Fame cannot be anxious. Nor. A rose. Which is beautifully.
Climbing. As they do. When. They have. Care.
Thank you. For everything.
A narrative. Poem. Of poetry. And friendship.
And fame. And asking. Is she. Coming.
They will gratify. By a reply.
He does prefer this little dog to that. Now.
So it was stated. And they. Will reply.
That they will. Kindly continue. To lie.
There. Quietly.
Thank you. For your interest.
A long narrative poem. Is commenced. And. Ready.
When this. You see. You are all. To me.
Winning his. Way. When. This. You say.

You reply. In this. Way. Thanking. You. To-day.
A narrative poem. Is made. On Wednesday.
And the day. Following Wednesday. And Thursday.
And continued as well. Every day. Except. Sunday.
Which is the day. When the wedding. Ends. Monday.
A narrative poem. Will continue. As well.
Because. It should be. This way. As there. Is fame.
Thank you. Just the same.
In waiting. For the name. Which has been given.
To fame. They are famous.
And this. Is the say. They address. It. To them.
One can leave. What. One. Has heard.
It is not possible. That one cloud. Goes.
In a different direction. From another.
It is only. In one going. Faster. And the other.
Slower. That it looks. As if. They were.
Moving. One way. And. The other. In the other way.
Way. Meaning. In this. Use. Of the word. Direction.
And so. A cloud. Can not. Meet. Another cloud.
At all. As I have. Already mentioned. In Lucy.
Church amiably. Or. At least. I think so.
It is a very cheerful occupation.
To have every one. Happy. With.
What has been done. By them. For them.
They being. Their waiting. And satisfied.
Not only. With the result. But with.
What is happening. And the other. Ones.
Occupying. Themselves. With the doing.
Of what. Will. At that time. Give. Satisfaction.
And. So. Any one. Being sad. Has this reason.
They were. Helped. To be. Asked. For.
Nothing more. Than that. In direction.
And so. They know. Usually.
Now then. Add. With them. To resting.
A head. Which is. There. Upon. The arm. Of a chair.
From. Which. It can. In replacing.
Be. Repeating. Doubling. Action.
Now then. Ask. Is there. Better. A way.

Of saying. It would. Be prettily. Written.
And what then. The question. Of asking.
Oh when the question has been asked.
And there has been satisfaction given.
Undoubtedly. It will. Be because.
The question. Has been. So very. Well written.
With this result. In their satisfaction.
They will reply. In the way. Of why.
Of course. We will do. Anything.
Thank them. Then. For. This thing.
And so. Fame increases.
A narrative poem. Of poetry. And fame.
Should be written.
Naturally. And generally. They add. Everything.
Winning his way. Is. What. They may. Say.
With justice. Of. This thing.
Of a long narrative offering. A poem.
Of poetry. And fame. And friendship.
They will add. Nothing. They will.
Happen. To be waiting. And there.
They will see. All. Of them.
Some. Not separated. And some.
Not with them. Or anything.
But not. Either. The owner. Or the other.
Oh no. They stay. At home.
Even. In the. Day-light. Later.
And this. In not. Because. Of anything lacking.
Oh no. It is. Because. There are. Some occupations.
Which. Demand. That. They should. B.
Staying. In the house. Where. They. Are. Living.
And so. We. Know. Everything.
Saying. That a narrative poem.
Is written. Is the. Truth.
This is. A narrative poem. Of poetry.
By. Which. Way. Have they come.
They. Have come. Unexpectedly.
And this. Is. Because. Fame. Perfectly.
Is attuned. To something. And.

They. Think. Well of it.

A long narrative poem. Of poetry. And fame.

Should. A change. Be made. Agreeably.

Or. In the cause. Of. With. Because.

They will. Not do them. Any. Harm.

This can be said. Of a dog. And of. A man.

Because. They can connect. That he is patient.

Because it pleases. Should they. Make a mistake.

It would. Not be. Perceptible.

In their employment. They do remember. That they have. No son.

But in their. Way. They allow. For this.

Which is. What makes. It. Not. Of undue. Importance.

And so. They may. Be able. To make. Fame.

A display. They may. Gather. Lilies. Of the valley.

Every day. As well. As sometime. In summer.

May they be. At least. Famous. Because. It is. Their boast.

They may easily. Not be startled.

And should. They cherish. The orphan boy.

His name. Would be. Edward.

All have reason. To wish. And let them. Wish.

Winning his way. A narrative poem. Of poetry. And friendship.

Which. Makes them add. What. When they.

Came. To mean. To ask. Them. To name.

Fame. Come. To call them. To be sure.

That they had it. Because. They can. Not.

Neglect. Theirs. As their. Result.

If you water. Weeds. With water. Mixed.

With. Something. Withering. Will. The weeds.

Wither. Or will. Some of them. Wither.

Will they. Not. Only. Some of them. Wither.

But more. Of them. Will come. Up. Later.

Any one. Can ask. For that kind. Of a.

Seed. And. Now. Petunia. And. Now.

Petunia. Can not. Be better. Than that kind of a seed.

The name. Which is destined. To fame.

Is. My name. And so. They thank me. Sometime.

And. Very gladly. They think twice.
Before. Neglecting. To. Believe. Me.
And so. They will say. It is handled. By them. This. This day.
And as she moves. The shadow. Is seen. So that. One knows.
That she is making. Tapestry.
What is the cover. Of which. They prefer.
Whether. They will. Ever. Bother.
With it. As a hope. Of which. They knew.
This is thought. Very well. A denial.
A poem. Of wealth. And pleasure.
A poem. Of victory. And. Determination.
A poem. Of interest. And surprise.
A poem of poetry. And friendship.
A long narrative poem. Of poetry. And fame.
They will kindly. Think the same. Of a. Name.
They will have. Their being. Theirs. Appointed.
Just the same. It is easy. Not. To be. Of interest.
In that. Because. Of their octagonal.
In a. Glow worm. Which he has. No reason.
To call. Attention. To their pleasure.
Is all of it. In which. They mean.
Their allowance. In readiness. And. Thanks.
He has quoted. Them. Innumerably.
And they. Might. Easily. Prefer. That.
They could not. Stir. From. Here. To there.
More easily.
Let us think. Simply. Of fame.
Are ours. An allowance. Pleaded. Especially.
The fame. Which. We have. Is expected.
Not. In the quantity. Nor either.
In its. Arrival.
A long narrative. Poem. Of poetry. And fame.
And. Fame. They were. Famous. By. Their name.
Their name. Was known. And it is. Certainly.
Not. By hope. Or. By intention.
Think. Did. It. Come. Or did it. Not. Come.
It came. Gradually. Very often.
Forgetting. That. They are. Allowing.

Adding. In arithmetic. And winning.

Winning his way. It is. Usual. To win. The way.

And it is. Made. Welcome. By. Them.

For which. They meant. Something.

Fame. Can be. Encompassed.

It can be. That. They are. Famous.

Particularly. When. They wonder. If they.

Are likely. To have. Asked him. To look. For something.

Which is. Very well done. Because. He is quicker. Than he used to be.

Winning his way. A name. For which. They. Can say.

That a narrative. Poem. Is written. In this. Way.

What would it matter if they finished it.

As they might. By themselves. Just at once.

They will not. Have it. To do. More. Than once.

Because. They will come. In the middle. Of it.

And so. They make no mistake. Indeed.

By which. They will add. Theirs. Alone.

Think well. Of finally. Just when.

It will. Be left. Carefully. To their. Arrangement.

In this. In the meantime. In theirs. Of course.

Fame is this. They like.

More than with which. Could it. Be.

What is. Fame. It has come. All the. Same.

They feel. Like this.

At no time. Should they. Suggest.

That they were very well heard.

Herd. How are cows. Counted.

They may. Be welcome. Went.

And. He did say. It would. Be important. To the biographer. To-day.

They could. See. Seem. In proportion.

This. Was. As if. A shock. Of. Then.

Who. Are hours. With. That. It. Was oftener.

Thinking. In their heart. Sublime.

Nicely. Known. Should they. Better. Belie.

If they ask. Of it. To be better. Soon.

They are famous. Anyway. And not. Either.

Carefully.
A long narrative poem. Of poetry. And fame.
But. She may be. Pleased. By me.
For theirs. As a spur. To liven it.
By their. Being able. To do it.
Fame. Can be caught. By her. Having taught.
And he. Hoped. To contain. In gathering.
Wednesday. As a. Syllable.
What is it. She. Has pronounced.
That. They will not annoy. Her.
She has. Adventured. That it is. Not.
To add. Another. To daughter.
And so. Fame. Can be accorded.
And. An annoyance. With. Strangeness.
Below. Beware. Betray. Rejoin.
Fame. Is their known. They damage.
Their interval. In which. They. Differ.
There is not. A sheep. Which have. Young.
Not yet. Till. Saturday. And. A little tuft.
More. On. The head. And sweetly. Look.
Aside. In pleasing. Themselves. With. A wagon.
And grass. Which. Has been mown.
Believe. Those. Who educate. Her.
To value. Fame.
It. Is very nearly ready. In. Retention.
All. Who may. Be delighted.
Make us. Of their. Dividing. Decision.
In what way. Is fame impressive.
In this way. It commenced. Not. While they. Waited.
Not even. Not ever. Because. It is. Polite.
They must. Be a wedding. In which.
If she had. Had had. An illegitimate child.
One. This. Was. And would be. Placed. Astonishing.
Insofar. Famed. As. In. Indifference.
Come. Please them. For this. With which.
It is. Hours. A. Treasure.
Be judged. By politely.
What is fame. Think. Minding. What. They do.

The thing I wish to mention is this.
It is not possible to object to fame.
A long narrative poem. Of poetry. And friendship.
Winning his way. A. Long narrative poem.
To say. That. It is understood. That they.
Mean. That it has. Come. To stay.
Gather together. All. In delight.
For which. This. Made to be. Right.
In patience. Feeling. That they could. Mount. The hill.
Fame. Can be. Marry. Mary. Merry.
To like. A doctor. Of dogs. Merry.
This. Is fame. She knew. His. Name.
A little. Added. Made. Beatrice. In. Chosen.
We like. To visit. Eggs. Weekly.
There is an alternative. Of poetry. Of fame.
She is. Easily. Asleep. With. Victory.
It is a pleasure. To hear this. Of that.
This. In finding. That they. Made. It do.
Next. I will tell. How. It came. To be. Fame.
A long narrative poem. Of fame. And poetry.
When. They. Make mention. Of why.
They will. Be sought. For.
Blame. No one. For their. Coming here.
Nor do they. Even. In their. Pleasure.
Leave it. For this. In a place. In. Which.
They may settle. For. Their. Union.
Oh very much. As much. Ever. Means.
Faithfully. Borne. With actions. Disclose.
Be. Considerably. Relieved. For. Seen.
For. Which. They may. Seem.
Made. Better. In. Disclosed.
It is. Not timely. To. Venture very much.
In calling him in.
It is. Very well. Named. A name. Fame.
Come. Gather graciously. For a number.
Hours. In which. They can care.
Believe. In the one. With whom.
They prize. Everything.

Come fairly well. To mention.
Should any one. Disclose. That.
And this. Rests. With him.
In which. They can. State.
It is. Called. In. Federation.
And thus. A name. Makes. Fame.
So he says. In carefully. Thinking.
It is very little likely. That they. Are content.
With the whole summer. In the beginning.
In the heat. They may have. Their harvest in.
Every one. Knows. How many loads. In how many loads.
They are loading. What they have. Been cutting. And drying.
Thank them. For everything.
It is remarkable. That it is. Fertile.
Just may they stay there. With them. In time.
Gradually. It has grown warmer. Just here. In this corner.
And this may surprise. Them. In flushing.
When it has been. A derivation.
That. They are accommodating. This to fame.
Are they famous. Because they have been winning.
Or I am.
A long narrative poem. Of poetry and fame.
In a minute. He has not been. Hungry.
But. This. Has not stopped. His. Amusement.
Thank. You. For thanking. Some one. For everything.
In their behalf. For them. Insomuch.
As beseeches. And trust. As teaches.
That beginning is winning. Furtively.
Could you remember me.
A long poem. Of poetry.
A long narrative poem. Of poetry.
A long narrative poem. Of their. Selection.
How did. They come. To say. That it was.
Perfectly. Ready for them. In. This way.
Thanking them. For sleeping. In the. Evening.
They made it best. In. Inventing.
Very well. They may.
Be famous. In. Every way.

Fame. Is a necessary thing.
This is. The way. It came. To them.
A long poem. Of fame. A long poem.
A narrative poem. Of poetry. And fame.
This is their name. A long. Narrative poem.
Of poetry. And. Of fame.
Fame is. What they. Leave. Added. In. Addition.
They will be famous. Because. They had. A dog.
He will try. To be. Famous. By having conquered.
And this makes engaging. In relatively.
In relation. To their. Not knowing. A moon.
A moon. So there was. Allowed. Is made. Of green cheese.
Purchase. Plain. Plainly. Pained. By their.
Misunderstanding. Do please. Make it plain.
However. Much. They frowned. Out loud.
They need to. Speak well. Of them.
Let us think well. Of why they were anxious.
Please comply. With their wishes.
Do not prepare. To have his. As intention.
Making it plain. Exactly what they think.
More than enough. Who do. Asking. It to be prepared.
A name. Is kindness itself.
And now. Robustly. To think. About fame.
Fame is their pleasure. Theirs is. Their treasure.
It was. Not a mistake. To make them.
In politeness. In their way. As they. Came.
To be along. It is wisely. Now. That they think.
How many. Cats and their kittens. No. Cats.
Have. Their kittens. They are. Divided. By.
Having made. A pleasure. For them.
And so. It is nicely. In and. For expedience.
To think. Rapidly. As. At once.
For all.
Fame. Which is poetry. Is this.
They will. Look. And theirs. Is most.
Without. An allowance. Are. Remarkably.
More. Than they. Withstood. With wishes.
A wish bone. Is kissed. And they. Are misses.

Whenever. They ask. A question. It is answered.
If the question. Is. What is that. It is. Answered.
What is that. It is. A spring dog.
And will they. Like it. They will grow.
To be very fond of it.
Leading to poetry and accounts.
Will they please. In trifles. They certainly. Will.
In this. In a measure. In a way. They ask.
To respond. Yes with pleasure. Because. After all.
It helps. Me. On my way.
This is poetry. Measured. By the road. Being.
Warmer. Than the fields. And the effort.
Therefor. In a way. More fatiguing. It is natural.
To rattle. Paper. Once. Commenced. And was it.
Well yes. It was. Even though. On being. Examined.
It really happened. To be. A match. Which.
Was being. Struck. Upon. A match box.
No one. Is deceived. By a sound.
They come. To be comfortably. Together.
Just. As every now. And then. It is.
Unquestionably. Here. And there.
Able to be. Undoubtedly. This.
Fame. Is a pleasure. To the. Beholder.
And they will be. Famous. By Saturday.
Thank you. For their insistence.
A narrative. Poem. Of poetry. And. Of fame.
Which is. Now. Attained. And. Mentioned.
A description. Of what. They thought of.
Themselves. Precisely. Enough. Hastily.
Stopping. Because. Of which. They ate.
A very plainly pretty day. To. Stay.
And settle. It. By the time. That they.
Are happily. Warm. Which. Maybe.
In the heat. Of summer. Summer. Having.
Been. Summer. In June. June. And heliotrope.
And a pleasant. Growth. Of tomatoes.
They never. Languish. Being properly. Tied up.
We like conversation. With strawberries. And mothers.

They are proud. Of having. Been helped.
To strawberries. And have. Given. Some.
Thank you. Have been given. Some.
It is. Very pleasant. To be suspicious.
And. About. That time.
Fame and poetry. Make. Them having.
Not minded. Being. Bought. And taught. A soldier.
Birds. And a. Dog. And the mother.
Strawberries. And the gardener. And. A soldier.
Anybody. Can be a soldier. If everybody. Is taken.
Thank you. Very much.
Could wood. And never throw anything away.
Counted. Could. They. Be. They.
Much. Which. They regulate.
If it. Is. As joined. They will think.
Well. Of which. With. When. They left.
She left. Left. Left. Left right left.
She had a good job. And she left.
Left. Left. Right left. Louise. Married a sergeant.
Was. There a change. Made. For. Rain.
Or was there. A change. Made. For petunias.
Having. Come to think. That. A word.
A word. Of. Welcome.
It is made. That. She. Is provided. With a necklace.
She also. Has. At least. All.
She is. A pleasure. To the touch.
She will. Have. Prepared. To distinguish.
Diminish. Yes. Dear likeness.
For they will carry. For they. Will marry.
For they. Will please. In just. That way.
A. Pleasure. Had he gone to the circus.
Not at all he had cut hay.
May is. Not. Her name. Her name is. Therese.
They. Will mention. And motion. What. They knew.
It is. Not known. To be. Their. Purpose.
Will it. Be rain. That. They are having.
And welcoming. Or is it. Not enough.
A very. Long narrative poem. Upon poetry.

Also. A long. Narrative. Poem. About. Fame.
Fame. Is their name. And now. It has been.
Very warm. With the. Windows open.
While. They are closing. Them.
Because. They thought. That it was. What.
They were wanting. And indeed.
What. They have. Is what. They are. Wanting.
A narrative. Poem. Entitled.
Winning. His way.
The great thing is. To be. Carried away.
By the. Time. In which. A pause.
Which. They will say. Come. Cousin.
And not. With. Without. Either. It.
Or. Precious. Treasure. They may. Make.
A. Reply. To their. Whether. And.
Now not to make any difference.
Thanking you and them.
A. Plan. In activity. In execution.
Of. Their. Intention. To. More. Than.
Make it. A principle. There. Is.
No. Use. In. Add. Attack. To. Menace.
For. Their. A cloud. Or. Their. A dog.
Or. Their. Or. At. The time.
In which they go.
Please call. It. Very. Well used.
For them. Or. Without. In. Incumbrance.
We will never go there any more.
After. He. Was careful. They. Were. Careful.
And now. As. Much. As. When. They were aroused.
Let. Three. Be me. And she. Will. Well. And. Spell.
On account. Of ham and butter.
Wherein. They. Mentioning. Never. Think. It told.
I wish to say. That it never does any good to tell about it. And
so. There. Is why. There is now when. They know.
Pleasures. A. Name.
Winning his way. A long narrative poem.
Of poetry. And friendship. And fame.
She could account. Count.

With all. With steps. Wets. In going. To. And. Fro.
They may. Throughout. Throw It there.
In. Their way.
Please me. For them. Should they. Manage it. Then.
What is. Fame. Fame is. Which. Attaches.
They will think. Of a. Melody. Leave. That. To. Be. Alright.
Fame is. A. Little. Made of. Which. Will. They. Think.
More.
Or. Should it. In. Remarkably. Should. It. Be. Forty.
Or three. Leaving more. Or. Forty. Or three.
As a hindrance. To more. Than. Four. Or forty.
Three. They may arouse. Foiled.
But. Which. In. A glance. Ignorance.
Made. Plenty. As a cake. I. Found. The cake. Larger.
Did. She. With me. Ask. Singly.
Thanks for that thing.
It is never. Who made. Hers. Not. Angry.
It is. That. They. Grow. All summer.
It is. That. They bought.
In. The country. Not. A raisin. Is. Bought.
Leave. Which. In. Mine. Is. Thought.
For which. Made. A merry. Which. She. Fought.
Therese is resigned. We. Are pleased.
They. Will. Be translated. We. Will be. Famous.
The part in which they joined.
They rang the little bells. To hold. Off. Thunder.
And they. Stood. With. The rest. In. Listening.
And no wonder. As they. Felt. It rain.
And. There is. No. Announcement. But. Is. A wish.
They felt it. To be. Their. Wish.
What is it. They ask. In. On. Their account.
Which. In. On. Their. Asking. They mean.
Like. And alike. Made. In all. Unknown.
Could they be called. Other. May they. Praise.
These. For their. Rarely. As a Mass.
So much is joined. At their expense.
And please. Choose. Them. Occasion.
They will be. Fashioned. Are. And arbors.

All. In a glance. She liked La France roses.
Winning his way. And she was angry.
She said. The water. Should be used.
As if. To wish.
What is fame. They add clad to glad.
And little ways to having left. As.
Her beauty. Never held us.
A bouquet made of three roses. And. The jasmine.
I am hopeful. That. I am. Successful.
Winning his way. A long poem. Of fame.
A narrative. Of poetry. And of friendship.
And of. Fame.
Who has heard me. Tell them to. Be here.
With which. They add. It. Is. As well.
As ever.
May. They be. With them. In their. And. On. Their account.
For which. They knew. That. They were changed.
In. And. In order. To manage.
It. May be. No disturbance. It. May. Not even be.
Jealously. Because. He. Has heard. That she. Has given. Him
food.
And so. They will remain. In. Conversation.
What is. Forbidden. That. She should. Be. Their. Name.
And. Without tears. As is often. An appropriate. Come.
When they can.
All of whom. Have little ways. Of amusement.
And said. And saying. Just with. And. Without blame.
They will. A chance. To have. A likeness.
But. Should. It be. Mistaken.
For them. Fortunately. Should. Be. Mistaken.
As. If. They would. Cause. Fear. Not of. Future. Nor. Of.
Caution. Nor. Of. Countenance.
Play. And. Plain. They may. Gain.
In. Often. As it is. Establishing.
Supposing one had decided by buying that it would be so
long.
It is a very pretty garden you have made me.
It is full of things. That give me pleasure.

I like. To feel. That it is. Even. Better.

Than. If it. Had not. Been. Made. To please. Me. As. It is.
With which. There can be. Nothing. Better.

And so. It is. Very likely. That it is. For them.

This. Would. They. Agree. That. They. Are. Mistaken.

And. She. Comes. In.

And knowing. This. She. Does. Not. Ask. It. For him.

What is fame. I know. And. She. Does. Make. A. Wrong.
Answer. About. Watering. Starting. And. Startling.

This may. Be called. Commission. Of. Misunderstanding.

And she said. And it was. Touching. We will. Be understanding. And giggling. Is never. Repetition.

And so fame. Needs. No correction.

Winning his way. A long poem. Of friendship. And fame.
And poetry.

It is. An allowance. Which. He had.

It is. Fame. Which. He had. And what. Annoys him.

Not. Winning his way. But. What they. Say.

Because. Certainly. He is. More wonderful. Even.

When. They. Say. Things. Contrary. To. His.

Made. The way. That. He is.

He is. Very wonderful. And he neglects. Nothing.

Even. To being. Angry. And. Annoyed.

And. As. He. Is. Very wonderful.

He is. Sovereignly. Winning. In. His way.

In this. As. They. Have. Been had. To having.

That. They. Manage. To mean. Had. To having.

In this. This. Whether. It is. This.

Winning his way. Is what. To say.

In. No respect. To. Day to day.

And it is. Whether. They. Indicate.

In. Unanimity.

He will not be silenced because.

With. In. Within. It. May. Be then.

That. He then. Will. Be with. Them.

They will be. With him.

What is. The origin. Of fame.

What is. The origin. Of friendship

What. Is the origin. Of poetry.
Winning his way. A long poem.
A narrative poem. Of poetry.
Of friendship. And of fame.
A little need. Of this. And wondering.
Of. Coming. And they meant. In. Arriving.
And without. Spells. And they. Contrive.
To mention. Thriving.
Made in. A motion. That. They will. Voice.
Their. Happiness.
It is useful. To be. Partaken. And with it.
They may. Be. In. Fame.
Let it collide. Allied. And. Throne.
She may. Be toothsome. In letter. Or. Better.
Let me think. Of vowels. Are. Allowed.
It is. This. With. Modestly. As fears.
It will. Be. Quiet. Yet.
It may. Be. That. They will have.
Meetings. Made. In. Union.
I. Will be famous. As. Known.
They could be. All. Around. Aroused.
In. Turning. Turn. To the right. In. A. Tunnel.
Which. They decide. To.
A long narrative poem. Of poetry.
And fame. And friendship.
Leave. Honest dirt. So that. Vegetables. Grow.
And a dog. Lies down. Beside. A handkerchief.
And. She. Comes. In. To close. The shutters.
To the sound. Of. Their daylight.
It is. A pleasure. To manage. Matters.
Better. In that way.
But she is interested in flowers.
Which they may have. To weed.
And they will. Fulfill. Lilies.
Not to be. Roses. Heliotropes. Or strawberries.
For they care. To have. It there.
With which. They mean. To be. Restless.
Within. Their. Meaning. He is tempted.

And in a way. Resentful.
Also uneasy. And just. As much.
And so. Known. Not. To sing. But.
To run to scent. Meaning.
Winning his way. A long. Narrative poem.
About poetry. And fame. And friendship.
One. Two. Three. Easily.
Six. Five. Seven. Four. More.
Many timidly. Have many. More.
But this. May. Very likely. Mean. The shore.
They may. Mean. That they. Will. Be more.
Than. The unexpected. And. It came gradually.
It is very well said. It came. Gradually.
For poetry. It came. Gradually.
So did fame. Fame came. Gradually.
A great deal. Of fame. Came.
This now. This poem. This long narrative poem.
Is a description. Of fame.
They knew. That forty wishes. Were made.
Before this. Long. Before this.
They also. Knew. That if. They were. There.
They would be. More. Than counting.
They would. Would they really. Be determined.
Not at all. With all. Timidly. As well. As. Flourish.
Forty-two. Is more. Than. Sixty-six.
In a way. It began young. In. A way. It. Did not.
Begin young. Because. He. Is uneasy. And.
They were a pleasure. As a pleasure. It is.
A long poem. About fame. And friendship. And poetry.
Bide with them. They will be. Famous.
With them. They will. Be. Very well.
Very. Often. They will.
Let. Them. Drop. The thing. Which.
They are. Keeping. And they. Will.
Follow it. For them. In. Leaving.
And so. They may. Do so. Very. Welcome.
She may be. Rested. By their. Sleeping.
Also. May. She. Be surprised.

By their singing.
Winning his way. By moving.
And the. Union. Of. Better. Saving.
She may be made. To guess. An. Address.
And also. To allow. That. They. Will.
Allow. It. To fall.
May they. Keep. It. More. Than they will.
As. Fortune. They prepare. Made. An event.
Which. They mean. As. They declare.
What is fame. It comes. Gradually. Like.
The rush. Of dahlias. And the choice.
Of their waiting. For. Tube roses.
They may be. Quiet. While. They wait.
For oxen. But. Do they. Wait.
Do they. Do not. Believe. In. Likeness.
For more. Does. She. Love. Paul better.
Or more. Or. Is it more. That. It is. Known.
As coin. Of. The realm. I am. Taught.
What is it. That. They appeal. In. An.
Extra. Chase. They mean. Grow.
What is fame. All. Of. The hope.
Of the same. And not. Astonishing.
A long. Narrative. Poem. Of poetry.
And of fame.
Will. They mistake. Their source.
A long. Narrative poem. Of poetry. And fame.
She. May be settled. In. Having been.
Made. Into. Being right. In.
No regret. For their. In. Instance.
This is this. It. May be. That. The moment.
Has come. Which. If. Not even. But. As.
A mother. They will be inclined.
To be attracted.
It. Which. Is a suspicion. Of the. Imagination.
They will part. But. Not partly.
Because after all it is convincing.
That he is great. And she is. Right.
Let her eat. Plums and an apple.

Let him. Eat. Currants and lettuce.
Let them eat. Fish and bread.
And all the other things. That make. Cake.
Was theirs. Hers. A disturbance.
He spoke reasonably. And authoritatively.
And they. Will know. That.
What can. Induce them. To acknowledge this. Of. Him.
Nor does. It interest. Her. To ask. An. Answer.
But they may believe. A rhyme. With. Achieve.
It is necessary. To have this. Given. To. Him.
Let. Those who know. Refrain. From. Saying so.
What is. It. To be. Astonishing. More than.
They account. On account. By. Rendition.
It will cause daily. Butter. Daily.
Have daily. Bread daily.
Made. Very well. By them.
A long narrative poem.
It is an extra help. With them.
In welcoming. Welcome. In. Having.
Have they fame. He has fame.
A long narrative poem. On poetry. And fame.
Hours now. Which they allow.
Theirs. As carefully. Correcting.
Have windows held. With. Opening.
A fair. Is where. They hold. Milk.
And other gifts. For. Purchasing.
It is easily thought to be alike.
Winning his way. A long narrative poem.
Written about poetry. And friendship. And fame.
Would. He wonder. Whether. It made. A better.
Intended whether. They will. Be whether.
Ought or should. Mention a name.
It is. It was. Fame.
Did she. Widen. The name. More. Than claim.
If she. Whether. It would be. Rather. That she.
Needed. To gather. Rather. Than whether.
In mentioning. The name. In case. Of equally.
The same. Their. Fame.

Or is it an account. Of. Extra tradition.
Do they do. Or polite. Or might.
Might she. Have imagination. For a name.
All the same. It would. Languish.
For. Their name. This. Which. Will call.
Poetry. To be fame. Or. May. They. Make. A mistake.
A long narrative poem. Of poetry. And. About fame.
Is it. A hope. Of pleasure. That makes them.
Let. Her know. That. It is not so.
May they carry. Their. Whether.
They will. Know. That. They. Tell them so.
Or. More shrewdly. With. Their pound.
They will. Make. A force. Or. Force.
Of course. In. Which way. Will they go
It is politely now. That they. Relish.
Made. By mind them. May they. Rely.
It is. As if. In a minute.
She said. She remembered. His name.
Thinking quickly. She said. It was. Fame.
Thinking slowly. They. Remembered. His name.
They will. If it. Does matter.
Make. No claim.
This is the rudiment. Of. Yes.
They will. Be angry. As. Yes.
Whether it should. Be chalk. Or. A lead pencil.
By the time. She. Knew. That. It. Is known.
Winning his way a long narrative poem.
Of poetry and fame.
If anybody. Whose. Can. Choose.
Naturally. Three. They will. Meet me.
It is best. To forget. An. Amount.
It is named that. It is best. For forget an amount.
Thinking. Of three. They meant. Me.
Winning his way. A narrative poem.
Winning his way a narrative poem.
There. Is. A pleasure. In. Winning.
But. They will. Have. A pleasure. In. Winning.
They will make. Whether. In. A pleasure.

That is. That there. Is. A pleasure.

Will it be a pleasure.

Winning his way a long narrative poem.

Of poetry. And friendship. And. Fame.

They may. Be cautious.

And which. Is best. With them.

It is. Made very. Well. That. Not. Any one.

Said. More. Than they said. Of them.

And this. Which. They said. Will. Leave. It. As said.

By them. More than. They will. Have made it. Welcome.

For them. This is the difference between happiness and content.

If when. They knew. They. Were. You.

Would they have caught. Whether. For them.

Nor do they catch. This. With a latch.

With. When they made. To gather. For them.

It is best. Made alone. He likes. To have. Been found.

They may justly share. Having wrapped. It away.

Now. To place. An example. With. Much ease.

What was it. That they hoped. For.

They hoped for. The welling of satisfaction.

They could be. Continuous.

They will be. For. Happiness. They. Will be.

For success. They will. Be. Awaiting.

It is. In no sense. A license.

Nor may they. Be anxious.

It is. Thus. They. Are surrounded.

Now. What is. Fame. And. Poetry.

And. Friendship.

A long narrative poem. Of poetry. And.

Friendship. And. Fame.

The little matter. In. Which. He pleases.

He pleases himself. He is. Avoided. By. Theirs.

Nor leaves. It. More. Than. A bestowal.

They may. Organise. Victory.

It. If. He. Or. She. May. Call. An. Ounce. A. Share.

Bequeath. Their. Share. In. Harbor.

There are many ways of spelling tube-roses.

None of which. Are difficult. Nor. Indifferent.
Nor indeed. Curious. Nor indeed. Merely. A. Habit.
They will. Plant. And. Imply. That.
Their arrangement. Has been. Chartered. And. Begging.
They will. Arrange. Mingle. With. Their hope.
And so. They shall. Not. Object. To. Noises.
As. They can. In their departure. Be. Hilarious.
For which. One. Sings. Really. Well.
A long narrative poem. Of poetry. And fame.
Why do they. Keep. Away. From. Description.
For. No reason.
Nor will they. Hope. To be. Famous.
Which they are. Because. It is. Deserved.
There may be. An error. In mistaking. Their use.
Of their name. They. Will be named. Walter. William.
In having. Thought. Oftener. They will manage.
To appoint. Their arrangement. With them.
In this way. Fame is the same. But. Not for them.
Nor. Added. In the beginning. Of adding. Obliging.
They are obliged to be famous. That is. Their. Meaning.
Thank you. For having thought. Of everything.
A long narrative poem. Of fame. And poetry.
Buy. A buyer. Think. And. Apply.
Their thought. To their. Meaning.
What is. Fame. Should they. Be autocratic.
They must be thoughtful. Of. Their. Men.
And this. May lead. When.
To be told. Made. As. Ten.
One at a time. Is. Caught.
Three at a time. Are sought.
Six at a time. Are nine.
Twenty more. May incline. Them.
To be precious. In. Or a quantity.
They will hope. To be careful. Of. Fears.
And may. They. Ask. Their name.
Which is never necessary. As it is known.
What is fame. And what. Is a change.
For which. They may. Aim.

This. Is fame. That they. Will be. Uneasy.
About. A very little hail. In. Rain.
And a very little. Rain. On. Choose.
And a. Very little choose. In. Refuse.
And so. They see. That. Their name.
Is known. And they. Do. Feel. Very well.
Because. Of their pleasure. In seeing.
The window being open. To be. Bathing.
They should. Resemble. Women. And. Men.
Even. Otherwise. In their. Establishing.
Their. Coming.
Thank them for singing.
Winning his way. A long narrative poem.
Eight or nine. When they. Can. Or rather.
When. They can. Be helped. To. Pay. Roses.
Who. Says. Or. Can they. Think. With them.
Or. In. A minute. They will. Aimlessly.
Turn. Around. To watch him.
She may. Be. Thought. To have heard.
Earn. Or. Own. Or welcome. With it.
Or he. May be. Thought. To make. Them.
Have meant. To have. Them. With it.
It is. Of course. A rest. For them. To go. There.
With them. For it. Because. Of. A. Tunnel.
So many. Have a. Hierarchy. In. The. Month of May.
And easily. They will. Be. A sergeant.
In July. And lately. A garden.
More. Than. They like. To play. Very. Welcome.
I have been thinking earnestly about figs and gooseberries.
And wonder if they agree with me.
Also. Do vegetables. Cooked. In milk. Or.
Also. Bread in soup. Or. Also. Whether.
They do agree with me. Or. Any. Which. May.
Matter. Also. Does. Their liking it. Matter.
Oh yes. He said. Oh yes. And yet. If.
They made. Him angry. Would it. Be. A.
Different matter. All this. Can. Cloak. Fame.
A silk dress. Can be. Light. And agreeable.

And so. Also. A pair. Of scissors. For.
The use. Of paper. And. Cardboard.
And met. With. Fame. Is. It a surprise.
To have. It gradually. Happen.
Or. Not at all. Who. Thinks. Of it.
As. Different. No one. Who has. Heard.
Fifteen. Who were. Rather. About. To be better.
Winning his way. A. Long narrative poem.
There is. No. Reminding. Refusing. Of. Inviting.
Of poetry. And fame.
They may be all. It may. Be. Pleasant.
A narrative poem. Of poetry. And. Fame.
Was I surprised. Well. Yes and no.
I was not. Surprised. But. Sometimes. Angry.
And they could count. No. For. Yes.
They will. Be grateful. For. Them.
One. Two. Three. All out. But. He. Or. She.
This is. What makes. Gallantry. Gallantly.
A long narrative poem. Of poetry and fame.
May he say. That. There. Is no doubt.
They will not. Be pleased. Because.
Of this. Rather. More.
Be plainly patient. You. Will win.
They may be. Glad. Of anything. Then.
This. Is fame. To be glad. Of anything. Then.
A long narrative poem. Of. Poetry and fame.
Well may they mark it. By their. Difference.
Or. More pleasantly. By. Their place.
Or. As well. By their. Difference.
Or. More nearly. By. Their. Thunder.
If. At all. Do. Be perfectly. Apparent.
That. It is. Not. A hero. To. Deny.
And this. By a glance. At a pink. Sky.
Very pretty. With the blue. And they will.
Be politely true. If. They feel. That.
It is. All very well.
Who will manage to be adopted.
What is fame. Earnestly. What is fame.

What is poetry. This is poetry.
Not. To refuse. To hear it. Nor. To take care. Of it.
Will it be kind. To know. Better.
What is poetry. This. Is poetry.
Delicately formed. And pleasing. To the eye.
What is fame. Fame is. The care of. Their. Share.
And so. It. Rhymes better.
A pleasure in wealth. Makes. Sunshine.
And a. Pleasure. In sunshine. Makes wealth.
They will manage very well. As they. Please. Them.
What is fame. They are careful. Of awakening. The. Name.
And so. They. Wait. With oxen. More. Than one.
They speak. Of matching. Country oxen. And.
They speak. Of waiting. As if. They. Had won.
By their. Having. Made. A pleasure. With. Their.
May they. Make it. Rhyme. All. The time.
This is. A pleasure. In poetry. As often. As. Ever.
They will. Supply it. As. A measure.
Be why. They will. Often. Soften.
As they may. As. A. Treasure.
What is poetry. That. They will state.
That. They mean never. To be late.
What is fame. That. They often. May. They came.
Winning his way. A long narrative poem.
About poetry and about fame.
This is really to blame. Will they copy. Their. Name.
He would drink if. He were thirsty.
She would admire. If. He were worthy.
She would sympathise. If. He were. A birthday.
He would share. If he. Were there.
And so poetry is not opposed to fame.
Winning his way. A long narrative poem of poetry
and of fame.
Could they. Be happy. To-day.
By. Cutting hay. From sunset.
To the. Break of day.
Nor might they. Be. Welcome. To stay.
If. They might. Help. With the hay.

From sunset. Until. They. Come away.
What is fame. That they. Are angry. When they.
Are peaceful. Also. That. They.
Are peaceful. When they. Are angry.
And so. They. Know. That fame.
Which is. On the way. Is there. To. Stay.
This is. Fame. Some day. They. May.
They are famous. With having. Gathered.
That. They remembered. His. Play.
Moreover. It is gratifying.
Who will choose. To help. Amuse.
Them. When they. Add. This.
To that. In. That. Way.
There is no. Account. Which is threadbare.
Because. Tapestry. Is. There.
They will. Met. To. Declare.
Made. In plenty. As. Their share.
Which. They. Dare.
What is meant. By which. Whittle.
It is this. That makes. Fame. Famous.
All who are concerned with their respect.
May they be. Jealous. At a glance.
And pleasant. At. A dance.
And joined. As. A chance. To be welcomed.
What is fame. Or poetry. Or friendship.
What is fame. They may be kind to me.
And so I am not nervous.
What is poetry. Blue clouds. In a blue sky.
With many who are sitting. By.
This is poetry.
And friendship. What is friendship.
That they mean. To be meant. Or. Sent.
And they. Will. A little guess. That it.
Is present. In. Their. Dress.
This is May. In. Their. Stress.
This is poetry and friendship and fame.
And they. Will like. To know. Their. Name.
With. Fame.

With. Friendship.
With. Poetry.
With. Fame.
Seriously. Meaning. Fame.
This is not strange.
That. It is. Seriously. Fame.
Poetry. All. The same. Friendship. Made.
With. Aid. Poetry. Friendship. And. Fame.
It is. An easy. Day. To guess.
With it. In. Tenderness.
Poetry. And. Fame. Thank you. For. The same.
As. My. Name. It is. No surprise.
To realise. Even. If. It is so.
Winning his. Way. A long narrative. Poem.
Of. Poetry. And. Fame.
Winning. His way. A long narrative poem.
Of friendship and of poetry and of fame.
Winning. His way. A long narrative. Poem.
Of. Fame. Of poetry. And. Of Fame.

SHORTER PIECES (1929–1933)

A FRENCH ROOSTER. *A History*

It is awfully pretty to use a french rooster as a bank or a pretty
pigeon which looks like a lady with a velvet ribbon around its
throat. Indeed a rose is a rose makes a pretty plate and a careful
survey of a very small globe which has all the earth on it and
little sweets inside it make it a satisfaction to know that 1930 is
not the same as 1830 which is not the same 1765. When everybody is alive they need not dive. Diving is a pleasant art so is
driving. Driving is a pleasant art. It is very curious to be cautious.
History is cautious it is very curious to be history

I

By the time they went
Where was the little thing.
It is a very little thing
That they gave them

II

Pottery needs the damp
It needs noise hardly at all
It is less different from porcelain
It is less well known.
Many have been here twice
Very often they come again
It is very well known
That paling comes from anything.
Which it makes it all better
Which it is by the time they have been
There where they have been
How do they like it
They like it very much.

III

They were surprised to know that the weather vane worked
not they he they had not only thought about it.

IV

A hope in season it does not really matter. They will have it any way that is to say it is never like that.

V

There is a difference between a frog and a bird. Not always.

VI

This is an experiment to see how nearly history is.

VII

All are cautious.

VIII

Oh yes he is very well but he is very apt to be careful very apt to be often very careful. You see how failure is tardy. He is not apt to be only careful he is apt to be cautious as well. He is apt to be as careful and then he is sure to be better. An erasure is our politeness. Thank you for being so easy and not at all with impunity. Not how often but how well he is cared for. Nine does come before ten. Nicely.

IX

They will wonder when they went
And she says she is ready
Which she is to be sure
Of everything that was to be done
By the time that they went to bed.

X

Other than this cow can you tell the difference between a chicken and Lynn, she is not so pleased although she is thoughtful and they are not so pleased because it is better does it make any difference whether they will like it any better when there had been more oftener which there were all the early time in which they had nothing to do with it either he wants his ball.

XI

The way to go with this they have they love to see the same
that is allowed which they make whether in reproach of any
doubt why they make purses purses are paper weights.

XII

Our by relief
In mentioning either
They will generously lead
In patience weather
They will make it be
Relieve their holding
It is in August
That they will be there.

XIII

Modify and why
Because of my day
Why will they
In a vain display
Of not loving either.

XIV

It is our old anger
That they feel there
It may be that it is
When they may have to care
Whether they meet me.

XV

It is a better indeed
Fought with this strangely
In leading hoping seen
To be meant lamely.
Was she to eat corn
Was she or was she.
She may be said fairly

And shorn of making
Happily she is foolish about brushes
And hollows in wood
Wood which is not hollow
As the hole is not there.
She knows readily
She finishes with it.

XVI

Be here all three
Together there where they
Are In a minute
They will be sleeping
He on a chair
She there he there
They will be there
Sleeping all three there
He is left there
She is more there
He is more where
They are all there
He is sleeping on a chair.

XVII

I look at the dahlias
They are very beautiful
They are all rosy except
For a little white
A good deal of white
In those that are all white
A little white in those that are rose.
Rose is not red because
As has been well said
All rose is not red.
   In the center there is yellow not very yellow enough yellow
so that it is not red yellow or orange yellow and yet not yellow.
   There is no white in yellow which is this yellow.
   It is agreeable because there can be blue in rose a little blue in

a little red not rose and this when it is fair that is when the white
is there

Makes it a pretty yellow and very well never yellow rose blue
not red red blue not yellow.

The roses are darker than yellow they are not white with yellow they are like the bricks which are not yellow and they have
in them red not yellow.

They are paler than red or rose or white or yellow. Thank
them for having a little rose not yellow.

The rest of the flowers do not need describing.

He is through because he can hope to learn what there is to do.

He can learn what they do. Does he learn that they can learn
that it is this that they do do.

A park is a meadow surrounded with trees.

A wall is a spot where they do not send them away from it.

What is the difference between a wall and a fence.

What is the difference between day after day and any sense.

Who makes oranges when peaches are here.

Who makes mushrooms when cypresses are rare.

And who makes windows when vines are bare

And who makes little things

When they like to be here.

And who has held whom

When they are all well

It is by the time that they answer that they have left

This is not a hope but it may be a prophecy

Prophets are mad with do you not think that it [is] just as well
if not better never to have them listen which they hear when they
do tell it is more a fortune it is very well to not be very much as
kindled with the thought.

Dangerous it is not.

She does know the difference between a chicken a dog and a
cat but not very well.

She does know the difference between lily and lily white and
tube roses.

She does not know when they are ready.

She makes everybody think of what they said

They are very virtuous because others are relieved.

She is very good because she knows it.
It is a happy day.

XVIII

Leave it to me
And I will do it for her
And if I do
It will be what she asked for
And by the time that they will be ready
It will be ready.

XIX

It is natural that they answer intelligently.

XX

About is a house with a tree
She meant to find the scissors for me
And after all it was she
Who found the link that was lost and by me
And I found and it was found and not for me the scissors
which he had lost but not there where she had thought they
would be.

XXI

He was naughty and he liked to see how old he was and not
very often there where he held it as well as before. Before is very
much better than they like when he does not need to be followed
before he held it there which is why he likes to sleep not easily
but very long and there is no moment when they wish they said
they would not now.
It is easy to tell that they would not give the dog away.

XXII

A dog is named Basket
A shell box is electric
Accidentally
A shell is a sound
A boy is to have money

But as pink paint is put into oil he does not receive any and this is a grief to him because he would have liked to be rich.

XXIII

It is easy to have victory.
Belts are worn
History misses pansies.

XXIV

She says no but is she older
She is not.

XXV

May be we do but I doubt it.
Nice and quiet I thank you.
Believe me it is not for pleasure that I do it.

XXVI

What is poetry, history is poetry when you get used to the french.

Part II

Many means many.
And they will take
It away from him
They like him for awhile
Which is why they leave it
Being left behind does not matter
In a way it is careful
They will not manage to have it
Because it does not matter very much
In a little while
They will take it
Away from him because it is best
In every way he will be pleased
Indeed he asks them for it

In a way it is very much worth while
In each way
They must be ready
To have it ready now
It is offered particularly carefully when
There is no use in asking anything
Which they may have in use as well
It is no bother to leave it alone here
In a little while it is all over
They will have heard that he left
Which is not ordinarily more satisfaction
Which is what they wanted
In every little while
Very carefully made
Near here
Yes
While here
She meant more
Than before to him
In very often asking it
It is nearly made more carefully
Than when they established it by the time
Than this.
Made for their sake
To plan it
In a little while
In going around
To reach them here
In search of it
In plenty of time
Made fairly well
In the hope
Of being oftener
Made easily longer
Than they had been
Chiefly for them
Might they
In three.

He eats a ball
If he could
Little by little
Not at all
A very nearly wedding ball
Only the week before
And they danced well
Which is made serious
By Saturday being Wednesday
Easily fairly easily there
In leaving all of it
In reach of them
Will it be all next week
That two of them get married
To know two of them
There are all of them
They are four of them
Monday is Monday
Thursday is the next day
But the first day
They are married on Tuesday
They are married on Monday
Thursday is the one day
No one is leaving them Friday.
They had a ball Friday Saturday and Sunday
They were married Monday
They were married Tuesday
They were betrothed Wednesday
They were betrothed Saturday
This leaves Thursday from Sunday
It also leaves Friday from Saturday
It also adds Wednesday to Tuesday
It does not leave them alone Wednesday
All this is the month of September and well if it is
Wednesday.
There is no mistake in having wheat on Friday
Nor in having beets on Tuesday
No liking for their adding wealth on Tuesday

They need to have it best and most on Wednesday.
It is easy to finish without asking will they
May be they do but I doubt it.
Birds with their wish
He wishes to go
If he runs
They will make
Parts of it do
By the time they finish with it
It is a mistake.
To take it away.

ABEL

I

Their nature is mine
Will it be a pleasure
Which they have anticipated

II

That is better

III

Windy is not weather
Rain which is weather
Sunshine which is weather
Dry wind is not also weather.

IV

A little dog breathes heavily
Which makes one anxious
She stays out to look
This is also bothersome
She luckily has not been given anything
This is an annoyance
He will water the garden
This is their carelessness

It is partly why they went
To have it mended
It is difficult to go farther
May be they will
All of it is very heavy in the meanwhile
A threshing machine tires
Those who are ready
As well as those
Who have to be ready
They are ready
When they come
Which they do

V

This is not better

VI

I want to ask fifty
To make fifty
And it is a pleasure to like them
They will be all well in their way
It is left to them alone
To be careful of it.

VII

Blame means does it
Halve means like it
Shoulder means hours now
Women mean like it
Who makes their care
To please running with ease

VIII

He was simply it is true
Ready to make place for you

Part II

She cannot say what she felt
She must change it for it

It is not better for them
To like it and be surprised
Oh yes that is it
That is certainly it.
It has been slowly recognised
It is a color white
And therefor it smells white
He knows what to mean
A color must be felt
A color must be smelt
A color is felt and smelt.

Part III

Do they fit chickens to food
Do they not like to choose
Nor to stoop in order to cut green food
Nor to stoop in order
To cut it for food
Do they like to feed their green food
Does this help her to hood
Upon a chicken and its food
Their food which is green food
Because this is for them
As they need it for food
What is green in their food
Lettuce and salad and green food
Does it do them good.
It does them good to give them green food.
Not dark green food
But light green food
They do not care for darker green food
They need to care for lighter green food
Which does them good

Part IV

He asked if he were dark like him
It was replied he had eyes like his
He said was he dark like him beside

He was told not so dark as to be recognised as dark like him
as he was not dark enough to be noticed a[s] being darker than
others.

He had a bandage on his head.

He had fallen out of the automobile he said.

His father had not noticed that he fell

But his cousin was there as well

And he noticed when he fell and told his father he had fallen.

His mother did not like it as she was still in mourning.

For her little girl who had died of fever.

This is a story of a very sweet mother and a very nice father
and a very successful and happy family.

The mother had plenty of sisters and brothers.

So had the father

They were all successful amiable and pleasant.

Part V

In three days they would be prepared

If longer they would be scared

That is the reason they are preparing

Yesterday to-day to-morrow and Saturday

Sunday is the day on which if they were too long prepared
they would be scared.

Part VI

Anything I see I know

I told him so.

Part VII

No nettles are not here any more at least only very little ones.

Roses are here now they are different sized ones

Strawberries are not here now any more

Very few and they are not allowed to stay

There are other things here not too numerous to mention.

Part VIII

He like[d] it and then he did not like it.

Part IX

The time to stop is when they arrive at their barracks which
is their temporary home

Part X

She called him

Part XI

One likes to have history illustrated by one's contemporaries.

Part XII

That is to say that each one may resemble themselves any day.
They resemble themselves that is to say that you can know
them every day.
The way they are they are like them the way they were.
He is not disappointed in Harry.
As soon as everybody is satisfied
They do think it is a very good idea.
He never heard of their branch
He never had heard of him
And when he heard of him
He knew some one who resembled him
A resemblance is not looking like him
But reminding some one who had not heard of him that he
was like him.
The difference between laterally and not getting frightened
by leaving.
He came in winning.
Thank you he came in winning.
It looks like him.
It is like him
They are resembling.

XII

If he moves his head
It is not because he speaks instead

XIII

Saying it last makes them not angry
First and last
They will be left to please us
Which they like alright
By making a little more of it
They make a little more of it now
After a little more readily
It partly lean it for them
They are wider apart
In whether does it matter
Hours of colliding
In it being not interesting
Butchers have meat.
Better be provided
In case he is coming
They will welcome some one
It is not undeniable
What is the difference of thinking of two words or one word.
He has gone to listen if there has been anything.
Yes there has been something
He will bring it back often
Why do they put more there
Because they have asked him to do so.
It is very touching to have individual beseeching.
And she came in as she went.
What is the difference between a wedding and waiting.
We waited for him they did not wait for them.
A poem is one thing
A play is one thing.
Sitting in a garden is something
Watching nothing is obliging.

They will always think history bathing sewing saving and
learning meeting accompanying and returning paper and balsam
and being tired running it is a disturbance may be he likes it but
anyway there is a difference will they do so by the time that they
will have made it or had made often.

XIV

Very nice and quiet I thank you.

XV

Part of poetry
A part of poetry
Part from poetry
Partly with poetry.

XVI

Part of poetry
A part of poetry
Partly poetry
Part poetry
A part poetry

XVII

He likes to know he has to go
If he looks like a boat being a dog
If his crowing has improved their being bought
The distant clouds look like those of Italy

XVIII

A pitcher of elegance

XIX

Bats are seen but now that the hair is cut there is no fear.
Herbert hurries to have fish fresh.

XX

It is wealthy to have curtains valuable

XXI

I never knew such good peaches
They have tempted me
And I have eaten two of them.

XXII

When I first saw them
I was dubious if they were them
Then I was suspicious of the origin
And now I like them.
They are beautiful and they have good in them.

XXIII

Ladies it does not come right.

XXIV

Field and filled
It does not do
To have them help.

XXV

Would he bark if he could not.

XXVI

You must do vegetables
If it takes a long time

XXVII

What does she see
When she closes her eyes
Green peas

XXVIII

It does not make a difference
If the things are not ripe to-day
They like whatever they say

XXIX

They like to work
That is they like to do it
They are liking to be at work

Because if they are not
They are waiting

XXX

If you look
Do you say so.

XXXI

The heat is doing the garden a world of good
Everything looks much healthier

FOR-GET-ME-NOT. *To Janet*

I

For-get-me-not. She planted two.
As rose in bloom. Which may be true.
They need to mean. That they will as seen.
Leave two.

II

For poplars there. They can. Share.
Houses. May be seen. As poplars. There.
In there. Between. Buddies are seen.
More than they can. With them. And. Man.
All boasters.

III

Should each be awkward.
Should houses be small.
Or should they be better.
Or should they at all.
Need to be often farther,
Just as they can state.
That.

IV

Eighty stretches. From here. To there.
Here to there corrects everywhere.
She may be counting. One to four.
Or she may. Not be counting. Any more.

V

Though they will be. Willingly.
Shutters have been carefully. Painted.
Not more. Than there were.

VI

Should violence be done. To time.
To measure treasure. With a line.
To often measure. Whether.
They will be. Mine.

VII

They must be without doubt.
Should it. They must. Be.
Without a doubt. But it. May come.
To be often sanctioned. As an. In.
Coming. Soon.

VIII

Left to alone. That they color.
If they must be. The same. Color.
Or else. They care.
To come. Oftener.
Should they be careful.
For. Or. For them.
In particular.

IX

It is easy to mark. Ingress.
For eight. Large guess.

For ate. A guess.
For eight. A guess. I. guess.

XI

Ought. Is not. Left.
To fought.

XII

They will be hours.
By. Midnight.

LEFT ALONE. *To Basket*

I

He was not. Left alone. To wish it.
For this. Was in a way. Made it.
To perfect. The rest of. Eat it.
For their sitting. While they. Made it.
She might think. It was. The things. That fell. That made it.
Not at all. It would be best. To leave it. Or to have it.
Should it matter. That it is. More. Than they like it.
To be seen. As rest.
For it. Is. All. Of which. He did. Not. Have it.
Thanks. For sitting. While he waited. For it.

II

It is not very likely. That he heard. The bird. Which one.
Or would it. Be thoughtful of him. To make it do.

III

It is part of a plate. That did not. Fall.
At all. Neither the one. Nor. The other one.
For it. Might readily. Be an. Advantage. To have two. For
one.

IV

Should a little be. At all. Small. And when. There were two.
And close. To a ball.

Balls are plural.
Of course.
In advantage. Of course. For a habit.
Any habit. They have. They have.
Let it alone. Any. Ball that is. Of course. Lost. Is not. It is. Not
found. Because. At any cost. It is not. Lost Because. It is always
there. Where.

V

She made it a boast.
That it was as warm. As warm toast.
Because most.
Is always chosen. First.
In further.
There. Diminishes.
Could he ask.
For what. Is past.
With them. He eats. His dinner.

VI

Should a choice. Be a change.
Not if they love most.
And best.
By. Request.
When they leave it.
As guessed.
Or they come.
Conundrum.

VII

Little lions have not tails
Nor decorations. For the winter.
Nor ease. In wishes.
No extra appetite. In saving fishes.
Which may. Remain birds.
To remember. Thirds.
Happily. Sings. Relishes.

Whether. It is ordinary. To be waiting. For what. Finishes.
It is just commenced. Thursday.

VIII

How are means made more
He works. As before.
It is better. Or.
Will it matter. More.
In the case. Of. Better.
More. Than they have
In leaving. It. Alone.
Now.
He did it. Very well.
As an instance.

IX

How can a nun be left here.
Which she has.
Been left here.

X

Our ours. All ours.
As. All. Ours.
It is. Known. That.
A lion. Can be. A dog.
Or. A lion. Can be. A lamb.
Or. A lion. Can be a lamb.
Or a dog.
For the use.
Of. Waiting.
For that. Which. Pleases.
In sighs.

XI

It is why they like.
All more. It is.
Alike.
They cut. It. Alike.

Because. Of.
They cause. Of.
The cat.
Or that.
It is a pleasure. To be. Selfish.
In their. Renown.
Or come. To stay. Here.

XII

Just why they wait.
They state,
That she which is. It.
Is not. Belated.
They just. Waited.

TO THE FIRST BIRD
WHICH THEY HEARD

I

They heard. The first bird.

II

They had already. Heard. The first bird.

III

It is nice having a white dog chase a white chicken.
As yes.
It is nice. That a white. Dog. Would chase. A white. Chicken.
Better. Yes.

IV

It is very difficult. To wonder.
Or better. For them.
To be. In addition.
Their pleasure.
It would be pleasant.
To send. More.

There.
But. To be satisfied.

V

She and he.
Go together.
He rather.

VI

A first bird. Which. They heard.

VII

So that. They heard.

VIII

It is very much their choice.
To leave. It. To them.

IX

Having forgotten. That it was. Well. Worth. Their notice.
They had been. Finding. It pleasant. To listen. To him. Garden-
ing.

X

He answered.

XI

They were immediately. Anxious. To have. Everything.

XII

A first bird. Was heard.

THEY MAY BE SAID
TO BE READY

I

More than they liked.
More than they liked. Them.

II

For it. To be. At last. Lost.

III

Which they made ready. For them.

IV

They were waiting. For them.
They were ready when. They were waiting. Then. For them.

V

More often they were ready.
With them.
Especially. With them.

VI

It is a pleasure. For them.
To be ready. With them.

VII

As much as they can. Be ready. With them.

VIII

It is very strange. That when summer begins. They are not ready. For them.
Because during the winter. They are busy. Occupying themselves. With them.

IX

Mine. One. At a time.

X

It is very ready. To be ready. With them.
Are you ready.

XI

For them. Or. With them.

XII

Many. Are ready. For them.

I

She said.

II

Are we going to perhaps.

III

Which they did.

IV

As is very well known.

V

That they think well.

VI

Of a king.

VII

If they had one.

IX

To be sure. She would.
Be fairly necessary.
To a king. If they had one.

X

Inasmuch. As a king.

XI

If they had one.

XII

Would have been. Not a king. Or anything.
Very well. A cow.

ORPHANS

I

Never think it better.
To have orphans around.

II

They can be taught.

III

And they need not care.
To have flowers sweet smelling.
Since they like pansies.

IV

It should matter.
To them.

V

That they are mostly pleased.

VI

With being hidden.
Not hidden by themselves.
Or at a time.

VII

It is doubtful
If there is a noise.

IX

Nightingales are never silent

X

They like bushes.
And trees.

XI

But the difference is marked.

XII

But not exaggerated.

ADVICE ABOUT ROSES

I

Many plant roses every year.

II

Many plant roses that resemble tea

III

Many plant roses like a dog. Ivory white

IV

Many plant roses.
That is. Under direction.

V

Many plant. Roses.
Which have been. Planted.

VI

Many plant. Roses. In. Question.

VII

Many plant. Roses. Carefully.
And they do very well.

VIII

Many plant. Their roses.

IX

Many plant. Roses.
In autumn.

X

Many plant. Their roses.
Very much. As they do.

XI

She has been advised.
To plant roses.

XII

So has she been advised.
How and when. To. Plant. Them.

A BIRD

I

If I asked her.

II

Was it a bird.

III

This that we heard.

IV

She did answer.

V

That it was a bird.

VI

And she was right.

VII

In her answer.

VIII

That it was a bird.

IX

Because it was a bird.

X

Which was not any longer.

XI

Heard.

XII

Which was a bird. Heard.

A BALL

I

Fifty.

II

Call a ball.

III

She had put it.

IV

Not away.

V

But to call a ball

VI

At all.

VII

She had put it.

VIII

So that it was not there.

IX

Where they had put it.

X

As it was a ball.

XI

Which they had had.

XII

Not at all. A ball.

BALLS

I

They love. A ball.

II

He calls. And drowned.

III

But was not wet.

IV

At all.

V

When he was so nicely.

VI

Called it all.

VII

Which they.

VIII

So nicely.

IX

Learned at all.

X

That he was willing

XI

To be gone at all.

XII

To live. At all.

TO
A VIEW

I

Heavy sighs he is sleeping on his ball.

II

Not at all. Heavy sighs. He is sleeping. On his ball.

III

A view is seen.

IV

And he likes to mean.

V

That the light is between.

VI

Day and night in between.

VII

And so the lovely color.

VIII

Does not make the view.

IX

The lovely.

X

Color not of dew.

XI

But of evening.

XII

Coming through.

A
DESIRE

I

A fire. Was not. Her desire.

II

But nevertheless.

III

It was not. Her desire

IV

Nor either.

V

Further.

VI

But yet. Whether.

VII

There was. Rather.

VIII

That they were. Rather.

IX

As she saw. Better.

X

That it was wetter.

XI

If they needed.

XII

The fire.

A SUMMER WITH MARCELS

I

Three Marcels.

II

Perhaps Four.

III

Who can tell

IV

If there will be any more.

V

One Marcel brought two.

VI

That is to say. There was. One more. Than there had been.
Before.

VII

The third Marcel.
Was not there.

VIII

That is to say.

IX

He was there.

X

The third Marcel.

XI

Never knew.

XII

The other two.

WITH PLEASURE

I

With pleasure

II

Surrounded.

III

It may. That they wish.

IV

In pleasure.

V

Surrounded.

VI

It could be. That they would.
It might be. That they wish.

VII

They will welcome.

VIII

Those seen. As forty.
Or four hundred.

IX

With pleasure.

X

As surrounded.

XI

They will.

XII

Please them.

CHOSEN

I

Choose

II

Choose. One

III

Choose. One. Chosen.

IV

To choose.
Two Chosen.

V

To choose

VI

Chosen.

VII

To choose. And chosen.

VIII

Choose. And. Chose. One.

IX

Choose.

X

Chosen

XI

Choose. A

XII

Chosen.
A little poem
Made at all.
To please. The one.
And. So. Please all.
Chosen.

NARRATIVE

A may be I
She may be why
He may be idle.
It is might with lend
Then

For this secretly
In rest of them
She might be happy
To have seen them.

It does make a difference
That they connect
Connecticut
She may be he
Who found it
Might be
Why they asked him
To ask them
As much as they did

Does it seem likely

Who is known that they will have as an excuse
That it is mostly pleasantly to leave it wherever they liked

Follow find from that.
She made an excuse
In seeing him Saturday
For a conclusion.

When named ten when named again
There are many foreigners on the street
They are behind which they ask it is so easy to mistake door
for a shoe.
She made a preference
That she did not
Accept what was as like

As their hoping to make it.
She will never say
I do.
Yes I do.

A narrative of shares
Which they make
By mistake

Once upon a time there was a war
After the war there was rain in London
After that they had lands
And after that
They will astonish no one.

After or
Who makes
Him happy
Or whether
He is
Not happy
By this time.
By having a house
With little hopes
He is not angry
When he makes
That noise
He dreams
And they will call
Him to wake up
But they do not.

Forget Hindoos for Sundays

This is an introduction to hours of peace.

If he minded leaving her
Who had heard him

She made a mistake in arithmetic.
She said but is it

This is why she sings to me in tapestry.

Once he stood
And they waited.

Part II

Praise bestowed on her
Makes him praised in beads
Beads of perspiration
In hoping for this
He will satisfy it

In pleasure

She made him see that it was fortunately she that was he. And
it is not curious. Everything that is not this is nothing because it
is show. How is it shown. It is shown in reality.

In not being reserved, reserved has it. It is mentioned here.
When it is not with her he can make no verses and this is why
because she is hallowed even.

Now in the wind.
Examples in it.
She is not only but also all.

Part III

When this you see she is all to me.

Part IV

A narrative now I know what a narrative is, it is not continuous it must contain that they wish and are and have been and it is
that they lean in and together.

This is what a narrative is it does not need to be in remain it is
that they include in conclude in into remain.

This is what a narrative is I know what a narrative is a narrative makes no speeches for scents it is in their heaping in not
hovering. Let me see how narratives proceed. They proceed
without present separation. A narrative is this. A play is another
thing, a play is lively, a narrative is not lively in love, a tragedy
is when it might has been something. How do I know what a nar-

rative is I know a narrative is one when it is a property. A property is not on the stage it is here when it is on the stage it is an adjunct.

Why do we go to bed later.
In arranging tapestry.
What is the reason.
That we have had hats.
Because it is better so.
It is a preparation for their narrative.
She will be sleeping.
Very carefully.
This is a pleasure.
In reality.
I like it.

TO HELP

In Case of Accident

He made it be relatively an allowance.
They made it be not more than for themselves
They were possessed and it is difficult
Not to believe that a lot
Should be held firmly.
As it is they made no mistake
In possession
They do not return what they have
Because each is in left and right
With them in integrally
Theirs
Thank them without a gift
They have the right in their possession
They do not ask mischief to be theirs as bought.
It was not bought it was ordered.
Ben and Hilda and their cousin.
Come here Ben
Come here Hilda

Who said Ben knew Hilda

Hilda and Ben may gather that violets are always better always better than a quarrel with their mother.

Hilda and Ben have met in leaving their own cousin.

Hilda

Who says she went to meet dogs.

Hilda says that she knew her cousin.

Ben.

Ben does not always care to be alone.

Ben and Hilda

It is not because of flight and delight that it does very much matter.

Ben and Hilda engage their cousin in conversation.

How much are they alike.

Scene II

It does make a difference if they thrive in asking her to have disappeared that is to say to have preceded him into the dining room. She in doing so is accompanied or if not unaccompanied by their dog.

Ben and Hilda are often without sought they seek the means to be perfectly at one at home.

Hilda and Ben ask their cousin to come. He comes again and again. So do they ask him. She says it is alright.

Scene III

Hilda and Ben

Who makes them

Save the dog

Who is very well then

Who do Hilda and Ben say.

Hilda

Please excuse me to my cousin

Ben

Please have them meet there

Hilda

Do not be opposed to their union

Ben
> Be very happy in the midst of it being alike.

Both together
> Thank them
>
> What can be the hope of their having half at one time.
>
> Two or three or usually.

Hilda and Ben
> They are very close together.
>
> Repeating a name makes two names many.
>
> May we meet a cousin.
>
> If a dog has been taken away he does not know his cousin nor
would he anyway.

Hilda and Ben
> They may be very often blamed for their tenderness.

Hilda
> He may have heard of me.
>
> So may she have heard of him and of me.

Ben
> It is always meant that they will not mention them.

Hilda makes them answer
Ben prepares to be very nearly perfectly as much
> As would they go.

Ben and Hilda
> They like this

Scene IV

> They are usually flurried.

Hilda
> Who has heard of it from them

Ben
> She may be careful of it as they will.
>
> They will be careful.
>
> There can be no difference

Hilda and Ben
> How very often do they come

Hilda
> They think so
> So does Ben

Ben
> They will be kind
> So will Hilda

Hilda and Ben
> Thank you Hilda and Ben
> When will you succeed.
> It is of no use to hope that they will know the difference.

They do know a difference but they do not mention it now or then which may be certainly true for them and for every one of them.

A BALLAD

> Could. Should. Allow.
> That now. Having. Dug. By him.
> The place. Where. If. A tree. Had been.
> Roses. Which had. Well. Have been.
> Made him. Be ready. With him.
> About. With him. They will. Be all. With him.
> Well. With him.
> It is no doubt. It is no doubt.
> That they hold it. To have been well.
> Without a doubt.
> Now laugh. With. And he. Will he.
> Ready. With him. To add. To. Admire. With him.
> All having been. Ready. Or. To be. Ready For him.
> What is a hope. Rain. With wine.
> What is a hope. A hope. In time.
> What is a hope. A wish. That it. Will rain. In time.
> What is a hope. A spring. What is a hope
> They will go to hope.
> They will go. To hope.
> It is a pleasure. To awake her.
> Or. Perhaps. Not yet.
> The ballad ready. Is he ready. Yet. Not yet.
> It is very pleasant to think about a hill.
> He is impatient and so am I with waiting.

In many women wedding is an offering.
They mean to be with them in theirs in place.
They may come well and be with them
With welcome. And yet no one
Should be without a trace.
Of their asking that they are wild.
With delight. And hope very often.
Not to be bewildering. Although they do have.
Have sisters as women. And brothers. As men.
And so they came. To be without a flower.
And they had and once and rather.
Must they hesitate. With all and yet.
A flower. Which they bestow. In mending.
Having let him pass. Having let him pass.
And he was found. Having been. Let pass.
Finally. Once. Splendidly. She may.
Be often offering. To entice.
And no one knows. To. Entice.
It will be often. That they do.
Connect. It privately. And by asking.
What do cows eat. How do cows sleep.
Enter. And may. They wish.
If you look through. You will. See blue.
The table and the chair and the footstool.
All painted white, if you look through.
They are a lovely blue. And it is better.
To say better. And. Best. With them.
Or. Just as often. When. They are. With them.
Up and will he walk at least as well.
As. A wife. Has. Mentioned. What she has.
They went to stay and they came away
And they said. They may stay.
And she went to see. If blue. Allowed.
Black allowed. A sister allowed.
She went to stay and meant all day
To leave weather allowed out loud.
If she could be comfortable and contented.
And they. Have seen. That. She was. Not a queen.

But strolling as. Temporarily. Remained.
Which. They may. Be. As behavior.
Could he be. If. His grandmother. Had looked.
At her arms. And if he. Looked at his arms.
And his mother did not. Nor did his grandmother.
But they may out loud. Have reason.
Not to be proud. He may out loud.
Have reason. Not to be proud. But.
It is his wish. He may be inclined.
To intend. To attire. To blame. To help.
And to supply. And to remain. And to go again.
As if. Made splendid. By their willingness.
To hope. He could. See that. It was not often.
And so a ballad can remind him of distress.
When this you see behave as well as delicately.

Will an oxen be a cow and step well before a plough.
And be ready to remain if they should care.
To help them there. He was very frightened.
And should prepare. To have to do it. With more.
Than if they were able to. Undertake it now.
A pleasure makes no difference. To their having it.
Nor does their having it. Make any difference. To their wish.
Nor will they hope. Nor indeed plan. To leave it.
But they will always. More. Than give pleasure. With it.
And so. It is best now. To hope. That a cow.
With them the oxen. Will relieve. In running.
May they be well and happy.
Once upon a time. It was best. To.
Carry a shot gun to prepare. For readiness
And this makes it be a pleasure. To prepare.
But they will wind and remind.
That it is. As well. As they. When they wish.
And so. It may be so.
They may. If they see. In the. Distance.
See that she is sitting. There. And working.
Pleasantly. As is her wish. And.
Her patience. She may even. Be.

Very much pleased. And if. A tree.
Bears two pears. And they are winter pears.
Will they multiply. Or may be. Not.
They may even. Not be there. And be thoughtful.
Once upon a time. They meant to-day.
They were selfish. And they were at play.
They met with oxen. And so.
It is esteemed that there is a relish for danger.
Who may be authoritative. With our stay.
With our stay. And so. They in a branch.
Need many. Their retreat.
It was grateful. To have bliss.
And so it should be with them.
Walnuts should be gathered. And oxen met.
Walnuts should be gathered and oxen met.

To see with a ballad to see.
To see. And to say so.
Would she listen to them. With her heart.
And with her hand. And with her best.
And happen to be faithful to the way
In which she could. Did she. To make it plain.
That they were meaning having. All as blessed.
She may be waiting. And while. And sheep.
It is best with them. To make them be plain.
In having all. Which they may cause.
Prepare it. Dare it. Care for it.
Say when will they ask for the best.
And so a ballad meets them.
Best and best. And they will be better dressed.
And so. She may go. Might she.
If she refuses. Or a pleasure.
The wonder of it is. Some will be there.
There every day. Into and on the meadows.
With their cows. Even though they are.
Grandmothers little girls or daughters.
It all. Is a matter of taste.
And pleasure in reading or saying.

That they are there.
Many make many mild.
For them. By willing. Wade.
It is all taught. That water is not high.
Even though the land is under water.
Nor indeed is it. It is well placed there.
They will ask. Who has been met.
By very many. Who prefer. Joking.
And terrifying an oxen by two men.
Or either either either brother.
When he came we asked him did he tell.
And he said yes they gathered very well.
What might it mean. That they had a division.
In this way it is not necessary.
As all beside. No one has meant.
And they with any wish. Hear. Sheep.
Only four sheep. Many more. For.
Their sheep. No one has more
Than four sheep.
A great many have no more. Than
Four cows and three sheep.
And it is very comfortable. That.
Nuts make oil. Fish is of no advantage.
And everybody makes. A pleasure.
By and by. When they are startled.
It is a pleasant day before they make it do.
And they like. To be there.
A pleasure. In wishing. They wish.
They have not been hurt. By any weather.
And yet. They soften. When they think.
Of one another. As they do yet.
It is not necessary. That they are.
One alike. For resting.
Thank you for them.
What should they all do. If they knew.
What they all do. All through.
And how they came. To have been here.
Even if they had wedded. With.

Which men. And women.
Should they make no mountains.
Of gopher holes. And hopes.
Of hills. Should they. Or rather.
May they be cautious. For the hope.
Of making it mean. That they had not left.
Surely they mean with which they meant.
But they have not to go.
Not with them. Nor either. Not for them.
All may they be. With. Or without them.
For them. And mine.
After a ballad in time.

She may be thought to be for thought.
And they will fairly win her.
He may be helped to be her help
And they will fairly win her.
She knew very well that she was well
She knew very well that he would win her.
And then. Might they. She. Having.
Gone. Without. And coming back. With.
Might she indeed. Might he. Indeed.
He might and very well did. Win her.
And he might. Be thought. To have.
And he. Very well could. Did he. And.
Would he win her. Would he. Win her.
She might very well. Have been. Seen.
And won. He might very well and did
Win her. More than. It might.
Which she could gain. Or else.
Delight. Or else. Or win her.
And. In the middle. It was. Missing.
Not missing. But not. Attached.
But he did win her. And kept her.
Because it was right. That he had the right.
To hold her. And he held her. And win her.
In which way. They were anxious to say.
That he did. And had. And held her. To win her.

He did win her. He held her. He did. Win her.
And when it is. On the day. When they.
Said. Very well. I will. Win her.
He did. Very well. On that day. Win her.
Anyway she was won. And won by him.
Who did win her. She was one.
Once when they saw. That it. Was there.
There. Where. They saw. That it was there.
It was there. And she. Was a pleasure.
He said where. And it was a pleasure.
And he did win her. There. Where.
Where he did win her. There.
Anywhere. Where he did. Win her there.
It would be. As if. An and a man.
Asked. Can. Can you see. That. It can.
And it was not open. It was closed.
And first he showed it to two men.
In uniform. And then. To two men.
In a common uniform. And then to one man.
In a common uniform. And then to a man.
And he showed it to a man. In uniform.
What happened to disturbing.
They might. Wear it often.
It was meant. To eat. A cake.
Little ones. Are beguiling. And soften.
They will add often. He did win her.
She was won. And he did. Having won.
Win her. She was there. As when.
If they say. To win. One as won.
May they be asked. How are many win.
And they will ask. How are many with them.
All four make four. And twenty. Or more.
They will think that white and blue.
Is everything. One two one two.
All out but you. They may be with three.
And so they may desire walnuts or rather.
Oil of walnuts or rather better.
Or else they may desire. A pleasure.

Or else they may desire. Either.
Or else. They may desire. To gather.
Or else they may desire. A fire.
Or else they may desire either.
It is an ever increasing pleasure.
To ask whether. They will desire.
The pleasure. Of wishing whether.
They will believe or rather. Back.
They may go. If we say so. He will.
Go back better. If he does not go.
Forward farther. And this is how it happens.
It is a pleasure. To have ballad weather.
It is a pleasure. To have rather.
It is a pleasure. To have rather.
Or more. Than better. Or more than rather.
It is a pleasure. To have rather. More.
Than better. More than rather.
It is better. To have rather.
Better. To have. Rather.
Or more than rather. Nor more than better.
And so they may be. As they mean.
They may come more. Than in a stream.
Because or rather. And in a little while.
They may and they may often they.
A little girl can cry when a little dog.
Can tie and a little dog can
Cry. When the cows are not dry.
Because they will be dangerous either.
Or look so. And so a ballad importunes.
When they can cry. Each one can try.
To be comforted. By and By. Easily.
A ballad makes it be pleasant whether.
A ballad makes it be pleasant weather.
Be be beautifully
Be be mine
Be be be beautifully
be be be be mine
And so they make a fairly well ballad

Which they may use as a refrain
May we like to to be all told. That they they.
Will be told. For them. All told.
Which may make it reasonably do. One two.
A ballad scene. She asked for quinces that they were
There. And she left and she attended to them
And there were there to prepare
She did it beautifully be be beautifully
It may flower. Fairly well
In the middle of a ballad a question.
May be a better brother and a better mother.
And one other, may they be for one another.
And so. They will be so. And so.
One as one and two as two.
May they be as well as through.
With winter summer and next winter.
Who made it be. That they always did see.
That all that they had. Would be. For three.
Their themselves and what they held.
Who held. A beheld. That. They
Other than. They. Or. Better.
Than they would. Or. Could see.
They may be better. It may be better.
That they could. And. Would see.
That everything they did. Would be.
To give to. All of them. All three.
And so he came over here.
To be cooler. As may be.
He. As may be. Came over here.
To be. With three. And now.
He would be. Always further.
Because they would be. Three of three
May be. A ballad is better. Than.
A ballad letter. Come to me.

To unexpectedly see the moon is very exciting
To see an eclipse unexpectedly of the moon is very exciting.
And it might but it could not other than it was.

Even so it was exciting.

To unexpectedly see an eclipse of the moon is exciting.

And she. May be. Said to be. Not very. Interested.

And she may be said to be. Not interested.

And so to see unexpectedly an eclipse of the moon is unexciting.

And so to see unexpectedly an eclipse of the moon is very exciting.

She may be thought to be made to be.

Very nearly fairly we and quickly.

It might be. That there would be one of three.

And very exciting tenderly to be often it in there

And very exciting. A sheep might be black and and a sheep might be a goat.

And at a distance need not be very exciting.

And many may be waiting for a child of three.

And nuts are shaking in a nut tree

Because some one is striking at the nut tree with a stick as is the custom.

And so a bone can be smaller or not at all

And a tree may be tall and be a walnut tree

And anyway there may be three.

And a tree and a number of sheep

And there are many more than three

And so certainly three are many more than three.

One two three all out but she.

And so it makes a duchess a brother.

And a basket a sister and a little one a mother.

And so they may be careless

And resplendent and silver and a bother

And she may be very patient sweetly.

What is a ballad. Three things and a cloak.

She likes to be her. And sings

He likes to be with be. And sings.

She may be the cause of a ballad.

A ballad makes strings and they pull her.

And she comes and she sings with her

And he comes and he sings for her

And they come and they sing with her
And it may be so for they can know
That a ballad this ballad can say so.
She knows strains in melody. Believe her readily. She may be
present fairly. To unexpectedly see an eclipse of the moon.

Button and mutton a sheep or a lamb
A bird or a button or pleasure or can.
May they be rather or button or a ram.
At a distance you can tell them.
A sheep looks up steadily and they ran.
A ram at a distance and they ran
A ram and they can see the two of them they can
A mutton, a button, Button mutton may leave
As they can. No one should accuse
A sheep or a ram. That they ran.
They look up and watching they can.
A sheep or a ram any one can tell them.
Because a ram is not watching they ran.
And so a ballad has been told. To be told.
That as well as they can be and they can be
Bold because they refuse to relieve.
May they all achieve. May they think.
And thieve may they think and relieve.
Who may a button share. They found a silver button.
They care. To find a silver button. On the same day.
That the sheep came to stay and stood.
And looked. And was there. But not a share.
Of when they went away as they do regularly.

It is of no use remarking that they have changed their place.
That he has changed his place from here. To there. In fact he
was not there.
A ballad in difference. And it is a pleasure.

She will be of two he will see it through
She will be of two. And happily here.
She will be of two. One two one two one two.

She will be of two and here.
It is not very difficult to choose roses.
By their color, their strength and their perfume.
Nor is it difficult to choose roses.
By their color their strength and their perfume.
Nor is it difficult to choose roses
By their color their strength and their perfume
Nor is it difficult to choose roses
By their color by their strength by their perfume
Nor is it difficult to choose roses
By the description of roses by the deception
Of their color their strength and their perfume
It is not. Very difficult. To choose roses
By the description and the description describes
Their color their strength and their perfume.
In every ballad one of one is two
In every ballad many roses or few
In any ballad roses one or two
Are what it is well to choose for two.
Who make it always do. So for you.
And Peter plants them. Or who. Two.

POEMS

For a keepsake in dollars.
Which when she hollers.
But he hollers
For a keepsake which follows.
For which keepsake
Keep for the sake
Of little she
Which or that hollers.

Which one.
One which has been acquainted with this one.
One which one which one not acquainted with this one.
This one which one

Which son.
Have been acquainted with this one.
But now it is all changed because I have seen it in another
way.

Little bits of poetry.
Make a happy land
Landing.
When they see the land
Landing.

What is the difference between a river and a lake.
None.
When is one or either one begun
Why is one a smaller one.
None. Not that which it is.
There where it is
Begun or not begun
One.
I have never seen anything look like this.
Not that it makes it what this is.
There is no use in accompanying a hum,
If a hum is a very big hum-drum, like this is.
Each thing in each way.
To-day to-morrow anyway where they.
Will I ever mind clouds again
Not that we have become
Acquainted
The decision that what it is is not the same does not come
from the earth or from above the clouds, for indeed as clouds, I
wish not to use it as a name because as clouds, the sun which is or
is not one as clouds. Not at all and in any way the earth is or is
not one as clouds. It is not another one nor one because larger or
smaller if it is there it is not around, which meant to be the color
through for you. My what a really strange thing to do. What a
way it looks.

An airplane is made
For this with this.

What does this rhyme
It rhymes not exactly but very nearly with this
A kiss.

Yes an airplane is made for a writer to write.
Alright Alright.

MARGITE MARGUERITE AND MARGHERITA

These three are not the same
They are not known by name
That they are not the same
Margita Marguerite and Margherita.
Margite was in love with the name
It was not the same
Margite loved and loves the name
Marguerite uses her name
She knows the name is the same
As the use of Marguerite the name
Margherita does and does name
Does Margherita put it to shame
By leaving it all as a name all the same
Margherita.
Margherita was not astonished by lame
Nor was she saved by the same
Nor made sparing by a game
Of leaving it all for the name
Of which she would have it to name
Just why it should be not the same
She had two rooms and was gone
Once twice and always was there
There where she brought it to bear
That Margherita was here and not there
Margherita.
Marguerite comes once a day
She comes but she comes not to stay
Marguerite can come and go away

Which makes be once and a way
To share Marguerite not to spare
Herself in the share
Which she does which she does there
Which she does which she does where
Marguerite may they compete
Marguerite will not be quicker and quicker.
Margite makes mean to declare
That she only she can she share
She can be with them with them with and with them
She will only she will only be fair
Margite can care
That they can show they may fair
Where she will when they do not dare
Not only with them with their share.
Margite has you in union.
When they may be first at first
And at first first at first.
Margite can be there.
Margite may make prevail
Be frail
It may they think it will.
That they may much enjoy
Their joy
As they will still
Not be vexed by then
Which they will
May be when they are full of their wishes
Which they alike
May more than never have made desire
Marguerite may be caused for which to send
She will like to call may they call not to mend.
May they like to call which they call or second to send
May they inquire which they have it lain down.
Margherita needs best not to lean or quit her
Because they may be thou or thousands
She may be willing leaned or lean which may be
To mingle for it in which they are like

To stand more than in which they were often marked
To be not remarkable.
All the same which sounds
Made with and tin with sin
Do you three idle while they three not idle smile.
Margherita will she be useful to the other.
Will the other be left well to her
If in that case that there is a standard
And she might be here when no one is there
Also she may approve approve those.
It may have an envy in time
Nor may they cry bitterly
But which may fashion but theirs
Swiftly as a point in time
Nor may they cross there
Many there. At no time.
And so sedulously it is a fashion.
Their in appeal she may be all
It is but well an occasion if they may instance
Or not at all. A call. By them to find.
It may be only well without intention.
Or wishes
Marguerite is a plainly finish.
After and all she came from there
It is alone a lane a land a plain
And not a mountain, a mountain a land.
A plain. A matter of which.
They had not succeeded.
It is not only badly known as mother.
She might they will have been
Known not as much a by and by
She returns readily all of which which.
They call hers hers.
Margite is made a fountain blame the place
Nor in which on account of in a placing
She had it made there. She had it paid.
She was not lovely in a glade
But they can sooner seen and mean

She will be well by flashes and not merriment
Or best alone not only all alone but known as well.
All how to be kind.
Let her carry let her press
Let her renounce which way they change hers
For theirs
This is not the only way to remember that at the time it was
no wonder that they could not choose whose was hers first.
Margherita may have a standard
Marguerite will be a choice
Margite has known what she has for which she has no liking.
Margite be very well spoken
Marguerite be lengthily the name
Margherita be expressed with them.
All of which have a name.
And no name. But its name
Makes their name which they name
Margite has a rare name
Marguerite has a name which says the same
Margherita has an Italian name so fame.

Part Two.

Angels kings and country places.
The three are any of them welcome to well known.
Margite Marguerite and Margherita.
Margherita if she lost you she lost us
Marguerite if you could do it alone it would be best
Margite if it were ever all it would be all
Margherita Marguerite Margite.
They may be chosen which is all to call
When they happen never knowing one another
May be they will be all in all
Never knowing naturally never knowing one another.
Because how could they if they met.
Margherita who does not look tall is tall
Marguerite who does not look tall is not tall
Margite does and does not look tall at all

Margite Marguerite and Margherita.
Why should they not know that it is so.
Marguerite need not come to see some
Margite will see her come from
Margherita is not anywhere away from
Where any one cannot come from.
And so they may suggest what they had
Or thirty may have thirty-nine
Or they may not have had.
How can they be careless in the midst of this.
One very often is heavy with bliss.
And so they will have it that they arranged
Very freely their not coming.
Not all of them.
Margite makes a mystery of dismiss.
Marguerite makes waiting wait for something
Margherita makes writing waiting
And nobody is curious.
Or should they be untaught.
She may divine that thought
That with which they may
Or should in which miss
Their thinking that they may
Be thought they have not bought
Which they will miss
Obliging for it as well then
Margite Marguerite and Margherita
They can sigh just not why.
May they be not gentle yes.
Margite yes can not guess
Marguerite yes can not guess
Margherita yes can not guess.
Margite four make twenty which she asks
Why should he with them be careful as he is.
Marguerite she may just with them ask not yet
Margherita for them it was not only why but with them
Margite fell fast asleep not yet
Marguerite will love to fail in sleep as yet

Margherita has planned to be for them in sleep and yet.
Margite and yet Marguerite
Marguerite and not yet Margherita.
She may be earnest and enthusiastic and not yet
With them as yet a dog is not a sheep.
Margite by them to be selfish
Marguerite Do be not their wish
Margherita She must do this to be well.
Margite full of failing
Marguerite But without which.
Margherita may come back to cloud.
Their entire existence.
What is poetry. Poetry is made mine.
Why will they change or exchange
Not more than at one time
Which is why they will be never mine
And so she did not mind it or what she said.
What is poetry too
Just as well as you.
Or not more than at one time.
But which is it when Margite.
But which are there more for
Not for Marguerite.
May they be careful of their earnestness
Or they will answer Margherita.
Marguerite which will they thank.
Margite but they may just die
Margherita But which they will do.
Margite Marguerite and Margherita
All little ways are tender ways
She may do better if she stays
Margite all little ways
Marguerite are better ways
Margherita but which she says
She knows how best to leave it for them
As they know it best
And so Margite will think it well
To know just when they will not tell

Marguerite which they disturb
Margherita welcomes more than any third.
And not three thousand.
Was she as pretty
Could she be pretty
Would she and pretty
Not pretty well
For them as well
More then as pretty
More then as not then pretty well.
Margite should meet with her owning
Marguerite should meet with her owning
Margherita has been either better
Or not better enough.
Margherita can meet what can They be
Marguerite cannot meet that they do
Margite cannot need to meet.
All which all through
Each one they like just more than that.
Each one. They like just more than that.
Margite should they be well without
Marguerite should have been stolen
Margherita should be as well as changed
Margherita may she not even be left
To be chosen.
Marguerite they may without which they choose.
Margite for them it is often to care
Not to care for them.
Margite who has not who has many hours
Marguerite who has not not only their hours
Margherita they do care not for hours.
It is always Margherita Marguerite and Margite
Who do not only without which not care for hours.
But which she may.
Margite can wait. If she sits and waits
Marguerite can and cannot wait or not
Margherita cannot be without forever ever not.
Or which she may in their hope.

Margherita will say how not pleasantly all day
Pleasantly a day for which she answers may.
Margherita but which pleases.
Margherita or which much.
Margherita may not be for them a fortune
For which much. They mean
Margherita may be fast and firstly open
Margherita never can come back.
Margite makes nothing of a blessing sweet
Margite should which she does.
People change but not from Margite to Marguerite
Marguerite she may not be fair to not be gayly there.
Or which she may as Marguerite.
Margherita may be exchanged for less
Marguerite may be less and less
Margite may be or is not with a without less
Which may be she will.
I like a long thing which they like.
They may be why with them in suits of grey
Margite she lived for green
Not only not before because why with no hope
But health in dreams.
Marguerite may have what they will give
She will not live for hope without it now
She will not be more rich than poverty
Because without a share she owes it all
She may be thought not to be religious
Not only from her birth but not without
It is not left for them to be without
She is not there but not without it when she comes.
Margherita has forgotten what color it is
That she does prefer what color is it.
That she does prefer.
Margite just a little bit.
Marguerite has not known
Margherita. It is often why they join
Margite Marguerite may open a furnace door

Margherita may open a furnished door
Margherita Marguerite and Margite.
May they name.
It is always be may they have the name.
It is very unkind to call a name a name.
She introduces their rarity.
Why often.
It is why they are wrong it is why they are right.
It is why they are right it is why they are wrong.
Nobody will mean to please be them.
Or unkindness.
It is she who may settle in a fact.
It is he who may not settle not in a fact.
Margite Marguerite and Margherita
Margherita Marguerite Margite.

Finis

A LITTLE LOVE OF LIFE

It is quite worth while to have a pen. And to look at all those that are for sale. Because each time there are different ones and it is actually always attractive. To possess them.

A pen is a pencil and I never thought about it before.

Which only goes to show that it is astonishing. I never like hats that look like that. And now it is raining.

After all why are they very much as interesting. If any one is angry with me now I am not angry with them.

Or which they like.

Do please not change money change.

She could be left to me alone as well.

On this account they have no need of me.

It was with which they planned of whether it is not their rest to come.

Often when they can.

All of it which they will like.

Buy me a cake only not if I do not wish it. But if there could be a cud. Or most of it they will be selfish to have them better arrange that they will decide.

It is of no use mentioning for others because theirs will tell better.

I have been have to be that they are like it I can resist that is knowing that I say I do not like it.

In this way I have come to think often however they fell.

Practically why they went.

It is just as well that they tried to mean for this for which it is used.

I can think of nothing as well to say.

She fought for this and all the time they were meant to be called there first.

Or why ever they could doubt.

All this makes a man clean for which they like it as hers. Or in a plan of their own account.

It is better to be very young than not so.

And so they will come better.

I could appoint them to have more as grass.

Just why they play as a purchase.

They may not play for which they will not do nor at most not at all too.

It is very often when they like it that they address me or rather that spoils it.

It is not often cautious to be afraid of singular in their place they may or may absorb it for which they knew or like.

It is after why they will be there together. I have often looked when I have seen.

I cannot think why they are made better.

And so not lose often made to take.

All this shows that this has been left and so I would so much like not to hear her voice.

All which is true.

With them with no inconvenience.

It is not only with them but almost for them that they were accounted as not having allowed more by them.

It is often that we do not like to pass by that spot.

She may be often used to any avoidance. Will she say less. All who have been have not been thoughtless.

Will she mind what they say or understand a field better. Just why they should not wish.

It is so often that they may. It is on account of an interruption. Or just when they like.

Once in a while it is very often that they like it better.

All of which they know

What is it when they say.

After all whose have they known.

All Wednesday it is all day early.

Or best not known. And so they love life a little.

With which they may often be well.

Do they think it is my way to believe them. Or do they think that it is only not my way to believe them. Either way they are not only brave just when they should be.

Coming to see them makes them come one at a time.

Or which they add they will.

May she or will she if she sees it he will like what they gather for either.

It is often that she hesitates when she reads.

Or why may they not be waiting for them then.

It is very often as they look for them that it is astonishing that they know what they feel very well.

It is always her kindness.

He liked it better than to come again.

But would it be better not to come again

Or would they be polite which they like

Or would they not observe this. All of it is what they prefer just now.

No one knows just why he is uneasy.

When should she care indeed when should she care for me.

And when she should it was very well meant and made selfishly.

She may be without doubt as well established nor not nearly or made plain. But when they are and noticed. May this be what they are inclined to do. Not without regret.

For which they need me.

They were all who were there made as well as with chances. The best is more for them.

An incident happens they are pretty when they are there as well.

Once more he left very much to them.

Coming often and looking very well and being anxious and leaving it alone and hoping that they will come or will they be willing to have them remember that they are not anxious at all.

All of this is for themselves.

I am playing a game they will be known like it for which they will very likely feel but not be annoyed by it.

Or let it alone.

Did she like what I did or not did she like what I did. Did she like what I did or not did like what I did or not. It is often not only deplorable but useful to be chained to necessity.

They did not come with them nor may they remain.

It is often fortunate that they will be there not only by themselves just yet. It is in a way not that that matters. All of which they are inclined to which they are inclined to be blind.

I like another one best some are so often easier with which to have it in my hand is not to have a choice that they will see or not at all their name.

Who has been heard to feel well a little more in places where they could. Just what does she say. She says she has been there for the milk.

Or mistaken. I do like you if you are welcomed more for me. Or likely as arresting.

Why should I write when I hear.

No not with which they ride.

It is not a disappointment. Nor like it again. I know who likes it.

Just why do you sit where you do. Or like it.

He is comfortable in my chair but I will use it later.

Should she be mine for this alone.

It is always hard to begin harder which they wish.

Can it be why they went.

She went where they did not wonder why they did not stay.

Bay away only they do not count them because often they are

inland. It is an authority on mountains which are held as hills.

They went away preparing to carry the dog to show him.

She may that is to say he may not be vexed by an interruption or will they be well.

They do not like to move it away hastily.

She for which she will do nicely.

It is not better to think well of more of them for which they delay.

She chose and she chose to do it well.

Just why they came.

They need be thought that to-morrow they will be taught.

It must be known that roses can be rejected as well as flowers.

But which may be that they will not detain them.

She was asked did she want to move or stir.

Should it be just that they should like it.

Should they or would it be what if they lost.

Why could they call cost accosted.

Or should they be will they be.

Once when they went.

Just why they said it.

Just once a day is all they say.

But which they do like not only which they do like.

For which they succeed at least.

Or which they went.

Good as they go.

Ours of delight.

She should call politeness to call.

How is any one to call it mine.

Should she be mine.

She could not think often how often.

She dropped something as if she had been asleep.

Which they could mean if they liked.

A little a very little and if they change their mind.

Once she should.

Just why they should.

He drew heavily because he walked along

Just why should why should they not.

If they could not indeed if they did.

She is as always right he is not a genius but a great painter.
Can painters be geniuses oh yes sometimes but not very often.
Not why they went but if they went.
Of course he likes what he did.
Eat your apple darling.
I gather which they do.
May they be colored cordially as yet.
Should they just care.
Just when to change sometimes this is a question.
If it should change to rain what rain.
They met just as they should.
Just when they change.
Just why they will if they will.
They should whatever they would do.

A little love of life she may be said to be all day my own delight for they may like it best not only which they do to best arrange their own inclusion to be my own all called, I called her to come to alike and like it as tenderly as most as when as merely as if not only their own wedding announcement a wedding announcement and happy new year does she like sitting with a little dog upon her lap better than anything not at all she likes better than anything which is that she likes better than anything love may be used at once at one time all of the time there is no difference between all at one time and all of the time because not only not only frequently but always which which when all of in at more than for which in foremost all at one time all of the time all that at a time more than can count by counting or they remember well that it is to-day which when they every day for more than all alike because not only not also but more completely than any nearly is why when they she if we say happy happy new year to-morrow for to-day as a way to be happy any day.

FIRST PAGE

Not politely added who likes no one.
But which displeases by offence.
For they named cherries as cake

Or which they manage they allow first.

By all which I wish to say that no one is disillusioned. Every day is the same as next year. When every day is here next year comes just as well.

Do you see what I mean. What a common question. Or which might they come as they wish to come around.

When one is no longer well known everybody comes around. They ask what will they have. The answer is just what they did not have before. And this is not true because there is no question and answer. There never is any question and answer. Never at any time or always.

What is the difference if there is no question and answer. Or are they not disappointed since everything is changed. Authors need not authorship.

Do you ask me am I not disappointed in jasmine and rain. Of course I am. The jasmine is white and the rain is water colored and the earth is water soaked and everything that is green is green.

In no amount of allowance is there any savagery. There can be savagery of which the savage is not savage. I do not like the word savage because it resembles too closely sausage. I have made a vow that I will admit everything. I have wished for success and I have it and now I will about arrange that I have no thought of change. But changes come.

Oh do seek well of well enough alone, leave well enough alone. After all leave well enough alone. It is very little not to have any disappointment of leave well enough alone. Who says I say leave well enough alone.

Just to say.

I like all who wish me well and all do except a wish. Bless plenty who wish. Add no one and no circumstance. It is very well known that you must write uphill to be hopeful.

Page II

I refer to what has happened. This is what has happened. Do not disguise what has happened or its effect upon what has happened. Oh do not disguise what has happened. This is what has happened.

I wish to call all call me. Oh say do you see.

What has happened to me. This which has happened is that which has happened to me. I cannot exactly detain that which has happened because not only do I know it but not only do I know it. Which has happened to me. This which there is to see is that which has happened to me.

Page III

Please be plaintive.
Of course they annoy.
Please accept acceptance.
Naturally with joy.
In their cause because if he needs to have thought that the end of the world is bought.

He likes to hear it said that very likely there is no bread or what they need.

But she needs cherishing with care.

Once more I am influenced by what I have heard. Hearing is a delightful thing.

Oh can you be cautious with anything
Or with each out loud.
But this they look alike
For this they make this movement.
But might they ask.
Do I either feel
Or like that.

Page IV

But which they conclude. That after all there is a difference between some and no more. And more and very much more. The difference is this, now I ask why they tried. Then I asked why they cried. They I ask if they might have had beside. More if I ask I do not care to hear it although if I am not told I do not listen, I even can insist. Upon hearing it. And in this way. No one is frightening. Anything that they call mine. Oh pray with them if they believe with them. That they will ask with them. Why they will with them. Go away with them.

Page V

I wish to say that it makes every difference either if they can or either if so if they can and not go away. In this way not necessarily do they stay but if not they do not necessarily stay. In recently go away.

So much I please and please.

It is different. When you discover. That when you are angry. In effect, they go. But also not no.

You can remember two things. Make it three things. When as a child you could get your way by being cuddling. When as young you could get your way by being intriguing. And when you are old and you can get your way by being angry if they do or if they don't go away. Three things make them. When this you see say all to me. There is only one loved one.

Page VI

Anybody can be touched by what they read.

Will they please pass weddings by. And which they plan before they wish to receive

Made as they will because they will not try.

Make it a change make it a change for him.

Let him not let us believe that it will end

For which they gather not only what they like.

But may they believe in fortune for which they will miss fortune.

Just when they gladly try.

To make no arrangement better

Than they had rather agree

But which they will not indicate

Made casually as a blessing.

Page VII

Would they wonder if they went out with us.

Page VII

Nicely allowed nicely aloud nicely add aloud nicely neither add or not add allowed and so they make very much of their

chances. It is very simple to hear them add sentences if you are
in front and they are behind.

With which they add aloud.

Page VIII

How are they added which they can be.
Each so busily which they see
All to call may they come here
He could often suffer beside where
May they like that which whenever they use
All which they can but do they choose
She may be like may they not like
That we offer to have them stay
No nor go away.

Page IX

I like a half a day on one day
Or a whole day on some day
Or three days on Friday
Or six days on Tuesday
Or forty days and forty nights on Wednesday.

Page X

He is as much as he can be
Just whatever he can be
Not that we please as please to be
Known that he would be he.
Oh likely most likely he could be he
Very likely just what to see
See but see as well as he
That he will not even be
Just what he should be

Page XI

Very likely she may do
Just what she says she will
Very likely he may do
Just what she says he will.

After that why after that
Why are they after that,
Why do they not neglect
To come to stay with them
After that.

Page XII

I once fancied that I did not know the difference between at one time and at another time. I was mistaken indeed now, I feel that there is no cloud allowed.

I wish to feel that I can clearly state that which they are attuned to hear but alas I feel neither anxiety or refusal I had rather add that.

Should you be so anxious if there was no one withdrawn. But now not at all nor even as ever believe me that I had rather or perfectly glorified that they should wish. I am going to have two actors and neither one of them by name.

Act I

Come one and come one at a time but really I expect and I receive a great many.

Act II

They will be fed and meant that it is known that all are bought.

Act III

In resemblance he tells that it is all taught or ought as well as he asks twice or nice.

Act I

An Italian tells his sorrows

Act II

A Czecho-Slovak meddles with machinery gently.

Act III

A pole says, too well of any well.

Act IV

A portuguese is deceitful.

Act V

And two Italians claim a clock and an owl and they refuse water and wine and they welcome doors.

Act VI

The french are doubtful about what they wear but they will easily add clad.

And so all four came in and out of a door. Two doors because there is a gate beside.

Act I

Fortunately we are not alone.

Act II

Fortunately we are not alone because of her and because of her son.

Act III

Fortunately they may help to get her.

Act IV

Fortunately she can walk

Act V

Fortunately for us

Act VI

They will act.

Act I

Ask them simply say it gently do you want them to go away.

If they ask them to be here they always accept them when they come.

Ask it of me that she will be pleasantly one of two.

Ask it of them that they will be mine.

This which I say is this. One way of being here to-day.

I simply wish to tell a story, I have said a great many things but the emotion is deeper when I saw them. And soon there was no emotion at all and now I will always do what I do without any emotion which is just as well as there is not at all anything at all that is better.

And so now not here but there I will do it as they say I do but not as I did but which as I did which I did as I did not having but do. It makes no difference if they have not changed as all which is allowed is rather more of course. As they mention will.

There is a difference between listen and I know they will but I have forgotten yes as distress.

This is how sound occurs.

This is my arrangement.

I am going to say. All appal wall.

It was kindly a detective story. Kindly.

May they come to make repairs plain. For which no we should better than I thank you. I could cook butter to-day but not raw fruit.

A POEM

I

Believe me when I tell you what I think.

But believe me.

It is not easy to refuse to believe me when I tell you what I think.

Or rather it is not easy not to believe me.

II

They like to hear others cry out loud.

And they like to stand and see others see and hear.

And they like to know that here.

They can know that they can not see and hear.

But anybody can.

And anybody does.
Does and was.

III

Does and was is very pretty.
Do and see is very she
Did and said is very easy
And they will for all of me.

IV

Which they may with which they will.
Rest as well as all until
Yes they do not without sashes.
Added very well with clashes.

V

I did not see them near.
Not very near.
But just as near
As they were.
One once with wedding made a glance with credit at once
they made it a present to the ones they were with. It was known
as attending when they were attending to helping in accidentally
never have to make it to them in their mistaken in. What is the
difference if it is or is not made on purpose when then it will do.
The better wider that they mind after the firm of which they
might be seated as if they had loaned it until they were through.

AFTERWARDS

Why should she refuse to go on which she does not. What
else does she remember. She says she never forgets anything.
The way she goes on is this.
Once upon a time she saw that their names were american.
And she said they were known to her.
They were in a way.
It is a strange thing one day you never heard of any one and

the next day they live intimately in your house and every thing.
It's funny.

Poem I

I like to have a home life in the house
I like to like whatever I have
I like to put away and take out what I have
I like to spend money.

II

When I like what I have it means this
That partly I am proud out loud
And really not doubtful nor have I been
That everything that I do will bring something in
Fame and fortune too.

III

I like to spend money on anything.
I like to go out and I like to come in
I like them to be busy and I like them
To be here with me and out there too
Just as I wish them to do.
Which they do do.

IV

I like it very well to change.
When I change suddenly it is very nice
Because if I change very suddenly I do not have to change
twice.
Once suddenly is better than twice twice.
When I change suddenly once
I do not have to decide twice.
We do not have to decide twice.

V

I like what I like when I do not worry
I do not worry nor am I in a hurry
If I am in a hurry I do not worry

But I do not worry if I do not worry
And there is no worry in a hurry

VI

Please like what I like does not matter
If it does not matter if there is no batter
But there is if there is a success
Which if they gather they will rather
Have it yes.

VII

Once when I went to meet a cousin
I knew that I would say yes of which
They would not like which of which they were insisting.
But I invite her because I cannot do otherwise
As they will change them not into men.
Or not but which they remain likewise.
This the first time he has failed in anything.

VIII

But which I like it but which
We often act as if we were
Not only why they why
But which in nicely
Fry celery in which poison is residing
Oh yes poison is residing.

IX

Like it or not as much as I do.
If I were made to name if they do
But which they call they say I blame
I am to blame that he hears his name.

X

Like what I do
Do you like what I do.
If I do
If I like what I do.

XI

To come back to them.
They are there where they are then
They did not finish before ten.
This was because he had been out before ten
Which he hoped he did not do often.
If he did do it often
We would know what to think
If he did it when he had done more when
She helped him finish men.
Oh yes not known to leave them
To mean when.
They like it not only for them
But as much as they could when.

XII

She told me the bird had a name
That he knew the name
That the bird came without calling its name
And a child washed its hands as it should
Without blame.
But the bird was frightened and dead without shame
As much as its name.
He was inconsolable all the same
For four days.
It was told on Saturday by a man.
Who stood while she sat
And tapestry ran
Off her fingers
As quickly as ever it can
As she is anxious to be through.
Because it gives her just so much to do
And she must be rested too.
As there is so little to do
Of course there is a great deal to do.

Part II

Think how many think of how many days,
Whichever they think of how they amaze
All of it alone by which they try
May they come first or may they not why
Shy.
A horse can shy not now
Because all the horses they use
Are used to a cow
Oh how can she think that it was right,
To use it every day just before it was best
To put into the ground the seed that pressed
Believe with which ardor she proceeded
And now she knows it was not needed
It was best to plan so enough of it was sown
She said it would and it was not known
That they could really not proceed to succeed
Made not only now but not known
That they could not need to put in the seed
Without having prepared the ground around.
Dear me how many can change everything they do
Just as much as they like you too
For which there is no mistake
To take to take to take
May they take or please make
Fruit-trees planted too to do.
If they are not planted yet
They will get wet
If they are planted too
They will do
But she knows now
How many a cow
Need not do harm now
Nor houses too
Not necessarily for you
Because before they are through
There is no need to.

I

Believe it or not as you like.
They may like what they do.
Believe it if you like
They will not mind it more
If they care to before
They do.

II

What is a poem for
To help wash a door
Every door has been washed before
And now every door
Is washed as a door
Before and after too.

III

I like to hear them speak
I like them there
I like not to wonder at all
Why they are there.
I do not often know
What they will do below
But just to know
Is pleasant to show
That they like what they do
And we do too.

IV

Imagine if it rains is it wet
Not necessarily in between.
If the wind blows is it disagreeable yet
Not if it is better than to have it wet
But not at all as much as ever they like
But which they please if they are always persuaded
It is of no importance to be pleased
Because if we a[re] pleased we like to please

By hearing what he says she says.
She says he says.
Some day not very soon
I will not describe a moon
But how they like it here
Where they may be here
Which they do.

V

Has she eaten all her orange
Has she smoked all her cigarette
Not yet.
Has she waited or is she waiting
Which is what is left
When it is not only why they could but did
Whatever it was better yet.
Why on no account.
Is it worth while waiting.

VI

Once when they were in and out and not often.
Once and so often
I wish I could describe how it is
To mean that it is not only if it is.
With both of them.

VII

But which they do or how
They may do or how
I like to know which if they look
As they do how do they which is now.
I could not describe what I saw
Whether either if I saw either.
If I saw either or
How often they knew how they saw
Either or a washing a door.
Think kindly how two Italians
One a cook and the other a husband

One a butler and the other his wife
Each one rather but I hear it as if
I had never had heard it before
Before which I saw
That each had two hands
With which to wash a door
With which to help to wish to wash a door.
With which before.
More slowly than the door.
What is the difference between slowly and lively
They are not to ask which
Not at all which not only not to ask
Not which.
Then can be caught that I look.
He drinks milk out of my pitcher
But that is not what I mean.
She has no way in between
Which if which I mean.
To-morrow may be true to you
Mario and Pia Pia and Mario too.

VIII

She likes to think it can happen again.
Oh yes. She likes to think it can happen again
But she knows that if she goes
She likes to think it can happen again.

IX

Now at this present time this is what we have
He can have what he feels and she is dark.
Not dark as dreadful and not only dark but just dark
And she is nearly perfect and she listens to him
And he is not dark but he has not been
What color are they.
Oh they are the color we like.
Dark and light.
And what do they do.
They clean everything too

Not too well but very well
And now what happens.
He having eaten too much and washed his feet
Has had to stay in bed to have his sleep.
Not when he had it but when he had to have
And so she said
She went to see why he was in bed
But she knew it already just as she said.
She said she was worried but not worried now
She helped him stay and we told her how.
And we were all satisfied now.

X

While she was well and he was well
They cleaned everything oh so well
That it is a pleasure to go everywhere
Even everywhere.

XI

And so each one in their time makes a change
And we are very grateful, until we change.
But this time we are almost really pleased at the same time.